Language and Speech

Introductory Perspectives

Language and Speech

Introductory Perspectives

Frederick Williams
The University of Texas at Austin

Prentice-Hall, Inc., Englewood Cliffs, N.J.

P/2/
W69

ISBN: 0-13-522789-5

Library of Congress Catalog Card No.: 78–169129

10 9 8 7 6 5 4 3 2 1

Printed in the United States of America

Prentice-Hall International, Inc., *London*
Prentice-Hall of Australia, Pty. Ltd., *Sydney*
Prentice-Hall of Canada, Ltd., *Toronto*
Prentice-Hall of India Private Limited, *New Delhi*
Prentice-Hall of Japan, Inc., *Tokyo*

Table of Contents

v

6. Sociological Perspectives

Index

| Preface

The study of speech behavior has recently taken great strides in areas where speech has been systematically viewed as the performance of language. The goal of *Language and Speech*, as its title implies, is to provide an introduction to these areas in a way which promotes their interdisciplinary relations. Thus the discussion of acoustics overlaps the descriptions of speech sounds, and these along with the consideration of production apparatus introduces the distinctive features approach in phonology. The introduction of linguistic perspectives, both descriptive and generative, is designed to lead from questions about speech production and perception to the contemporary questions raised in psycholinguistics and sociolinguistics.

No text this size could report adequately the contemporary knowledge which we command in the above areas. But it does seem reasonable—and this text makes the attempt—to serve an introductory role. Hopefully it will equip the reader with some of the necessary terminology, bibliography, and even the appetite to pursue the literature of these areas.

Accordingly, *Language and Speech: Introductory Perspectives* is designed as a supplementary text for those students whose studies have led them to the consideration of speech or language behavior. Whether their main courses of study be in psychology, sociology, anthropology, linguistics, or speech itself, *Language and Speech* aims at introducing students to perspectives which have grown from contributions in each of these disciplines. A modest hope is that it will encourage students to make contributions of their own.

I am especially indebted to Charles Cairns, a former Texas colleague, now with Queens College, for his assistance in the many phases of producing this book. He is the coauthor of Chapter

3, Phonological Perspectives. I am also indebted to John W. Bowers for his review of the first draft manuscript. Finally, Mrs. Cheryl Steel should be credited for her efficiency in preparing the final typed manuscript.

Frederick Williams
Austin, Texas

Language and Speech

Introductory Perspectives

1 | Some Preliminaries

To many it may seem novel to consider speech as the topic of scientific study. One reason is that it is so much an everyday, taken-for-granted behavior that we seldom consider the need for its description or explanation. Another reason is that the scientific study of speech is so fragmented among different disciplines that overall perspectives are seldom described in any unified form. The latter problem served as the motive for this book—*to bring together an introduction to the major perspectives on the study of speech behavior.*

The Perspectives in Overview

An assumption underlying the perspectives discussed in this book is that speech is essentially language performance. Without going too far into the topic at this point, let us consider that humans in the course of their growth and maturation acquire a kind of knowledge which enables them to associate sounds with meanings. We call this knowledge *language.* We can try to describe this knowledge by the identifications of sounds and the rules which associate sounds and patterns of sounds with meanings. Although this is the description of language, it is not the description of how we behave with language. Our performance involving this knowledge is *speech.*

When we describe speech we go beyond the description of language in the attempt to account for all of the additional factors incorporated in language performance—the physical nature of sounds, the human capability for articulating and receiving speech sounds, how linguistic knowledge governs linguistic performance, and how such performance varies according to speaker and situation. Speech, then, is the complex combination of many factors, of which language is but one factor. These factors are the perspectives discussed in this book, namely:

> the acoustics of speech
> the sounds or phonology of language
> descriptions of language
> the psychological view of speech
> the sociological view of speech

For introductory purposes, let us consider these perspectives in capsule form.

The acoustics of speech. As speech exists outside of the human organism, it is a form of energy: sound waves. It is not difficult to study this aspect of speech so long as we have the capabilities for understanding *acoustics:* the science of sounds. In Chapter 2 we will see how sounds can be described in terms of their physical or *spectral* characteristics. Each of these characteristics has psychological correlates in what we hear as combinations of pitch, loudness, and the temporal qualities of sounds—or more practically, what we hear as the patterns of sounds. Acoustics provides us with the perspective on the physical nature of speech.

Phonology. Only some portions of the acoustic patterns produced by the vocal mechanism are relevant to the basic sound patterns of a language. In Chapter 3 we discuss the *distinctive features* theory as a strategy for classifying the sounds of speech in terms of the individual features by which we may differentiate them. This theory is also useful in that it draws upon a close association between these minimal sounds and the articulatory behavior of the vocal organs. Further, this theory aids us in speculations about how we perceive the sounds of speech. The distinctive features theory provides us with a perspective on what we call the *phonological* aspect of language.

Language. As we have already said, speech is the performance of language. To consider the nature of language, or the nature of the knowledge which relates sounds and meanings, we turn in Chapter 4 to two contrasting views. One of these, called *descriptive linguistics*, represents schemes for the identification and classification of sounds and sound patterns that have correlations with meanings. The second view, *generative grammar*, is a theoretical view whereby the relations between sounds and meanings are specified by rules. Again, we consider that a person's knowledge of his language is one of the main factors in speech behavior. Our study of this factor is the linguistic perspective in speech study.

The psychological view. Why and how can the speaker-listener use language? Vastly differing theories have been proposed to answer this question. Chapter 5 presents brief descriptions of three such theories. The first theory is *behavioristic*, where speech is seen only as stimulus-response behavior. The second is *mediational*, a form of behavioristic theory where an attempt is made to account for the processes within the organism which internally link stimulus and response behavior. The third is *cognitive*, where primary stress is placed upon the deduction of mental processes which are thought to underlie the creation and understanding of utterances. These theories represent psychological perspectives on the behavior of the language user.

The sociological view. Neither language acquisition nor language behavior occurs in a social vacuum. In fact, both are inextricably tied to the social roles and situations of the speaker-listener. Why and how language and social variables interrelate is the question of this area of study. Much of the activity on this question has been focused on those aspects of language which vary in different social situations, and on ways to classify the relevant characteristics of social situations themselves. We have called this area of study the *sociological* perspective.

The Overall View: Promises and Pitfalls

The foregoing perspectives which constitute the chapters of this book illustrate marked differences not just in topical matter but in the nature of the materials themselves. These differences reflect the fragmented state of speech study.

If we were to give a thorough account for the apparently simple act of one person saying "Good morning" to another, we would need to draw from every perspective discussed in this text.

Surely even then our explanation would be deficient. There is a kind of centripetal impetus or "a need for pulling together," which demands that we draw from these different perspectives to provide coherent accounts of speech behavior. Yet, as we draw from the different perspectives there is an almost opposite, centrifugal, effect. Information on acoustic and sociological aspects of speech come from far different types of research efforts, not to mention publications. Whereas acoustic phenomenon are quite well known and predictable upon the basis of "well-behaved" theories, we encounter competing theories within linguistics and psychology, and hardly any theory at all in the sociology of language. In short, the theoretical territory is not only unevenly explored, but much of it may be inaccurately mapped as well.

At best we can assume that our map of speech behavior will have to account for acoustic, linguistic, psychological, and sociological territories of theory. It remains for us to be aware of the boundaries of these areas and to seek contributions from contemporary and future research.

2 | Acoustic
Perspectives

As we said in Chapter 1, speech in its most directly observable state is complex sound-wave patterns. We can study speech in terms of these patterns, but this requires some knowledge of the physical characteristics of sounds—that is, of acoustics.

Sound Wave Characteristics

To understand acoustic characteristics, we must recognize that sound is essentially a molecular wave-like motion, describable in physical terms. Although these basic physical characteristics can be first described in terms of simplified views of sound waves we will eventually see how the relatively simple characteristics of sound combine into highly complex patterns in a time continuum. It is an understanding of these complex patterns that underlies an understanding of the sounds of speech.

Simple Waves

Compression and rarefaction. The best way to visualize the nature of sound waves is to think of a spring such as is shown in figure 2.1 (if you ever had a "Slinky" spring, this would be a good example). Suppose that this spring were suspended such that if we tapped end *A*, a few of the coils would compress. Then, as these coils spring out, they would compress another few coils together,

5

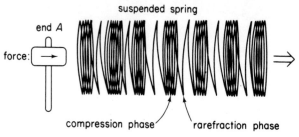

Figure 2.1 Spring analogy of the acoustic wave.

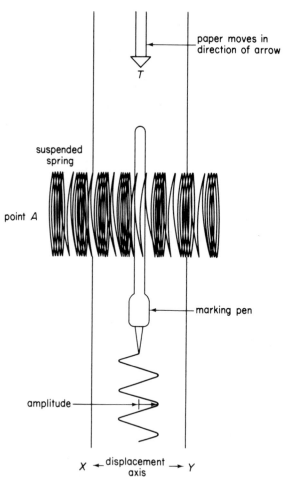

Figure 2.2 Illustration of wave shape from the spring analogy.

and so on, until these successive compressions and expansions traveled the length of the spring. This is very much the way that sound waves travel in air. Air has an elastic quality such that if its molecules are compressed (by a disturbance akin to tapping the spring at A), they will spring apart in a rarefaction (expansion) phase, which in turn causes a compression phase, and so on. These phases of compression and rarefaction radiate from a sound source and constitute the makeup of sound waves. We can describe such waves in terms of specific physical characteristics. One characteristic is the speed of sound waves, which is about 1130 feet per second or roughly 770 miles per hour (at sea level and 70°F). It is important to understand, however, that it is the wave disturbance, and not the air medium, that radiates at this speed from the sound source. The molecules of the air, like the coils of the spring, only vibrate back and forth as a function of this wave motion.

Wave shape. A way to describe sound wave motion can be seen in figure 2.2. Note that we have added to our spring a marking pen which is fixed at a given point to the spring's coils. If we were to strike the spring again at point A, and thus have a wave travel the length of the spring, we would observe the pen only moving back and forth with the compression and expansion phase of the wave. We could record this wave motion by placing a length of moving paper at the tip of the pen. If we repeatedly displace the spring at point A, and the pen moves back and forth along line X–Y while the paper moves in direction T, the pen will draw a wave-like curve along the paper. The form of this curve is called a *wave shape*, and its characteristics provide a useful basis for the description of sound waves. These wave shapes are similar to those displayed on an oscilloscope presentation of a sound wave (Fig. 2.3).

Amplitude. As we more violently disturb the air, phases of compression and rarefaction increase in displacement. In figure 2.2 this is illustrated by an increased displacement of the pen back and forth along the line X–Y. The maximum displacement corresponds to the *amplitude* of a sound wave. The greater the amplitude, the greater the distance between the top and the bottom of the wave as measured along the X–Y continuum. These differences in amplitude can be seen in the different sound wave forms which can be seen on an oscilloscope as illustrated in figure 2.3. Thus, for example, the wave shown in 2.3a is of greater amplitude

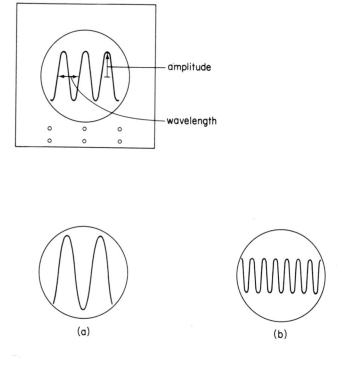

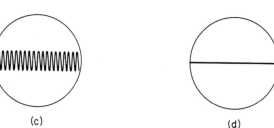

Figure 2.3 Wave presentation as on an oscilloscope.

than in 2.3b; or the wave in figure 2.3b is of greater amplitude than
the wave in 2.3c. The presentation in 2.3d has no amplitude at all;
in fact, a wave does not exist because there is no amplitude.

Frequency. Another basic characteristic of sound waves
is frequency. We can illustrate sound frequency by returning to
the spring example in figure 2.2. The more we would speed up the

successive tapping of the spring at point *A*, the more points of compression and expansion would simultaneously travel down the spring. If the paper is moving in direction *T* at a constant rate, the more frequently we tapped the spring at point *A*, the more frequently the pen would travel back and forth across the *X–Y* axis in given units of *T*. Accordingly, the greater the frequency, the more waves in a given unit of time. We can see this effect on the oscilloscope presentations of sound waves in figure 2.3. Wave form 2.3a is of lower frequency than wave form 2.3b; or wave form 2.3b is of lower frequency than wave form 2.3c. Frequency is measured in *cycles per second* (or *Hertz*) which refers to the number of complete recurrences of a basic wave—compression and rarefaction—in a second's time. Accordingly, a low frequency wave has a low number of cycles per second, or a high frequency wave, a high number of cycles per second.

Wavelength. As the frequency of sound increases, more waves are incorporated in a given unit of time. Because of the constant speed of sound, it stands to reason that the shape of these waves will have to become more compressed (as was shown in figure 2.3). One way to describe these shape and frequency variations is in terms of *wavelength.* Wavelength is the linear distance from one point on a wave to that same point on the next wave. We describe wavelength in distance terms. For example, if we are listening to a 1000 cycle sound, the length between common points on waves is roughly 14 inches; or the wavelength of a 100 cycle sound is approximately 11.3 feet. Figure 2.3 illustrates how we can note wavelength on an oscilloscope.

Frequency and wavelength interrelations. We can express the interrelations among wavelength *(L)*, frequency *(F)*, and sound velocity *(V)* in terms of the following versions of the same equation:

$$L = V/F \qquad F = V/L \qquad V = F \times L$$

Of course, the units in the equation must be expressed in a common time measurement (e.g., seconds) and a common distance measurement (feet, centimeters, etc.). If you think through the above equation, it should be easy to remember the interrelation between wavelength *(L)* and frequency *(F)*, since velocity is a constant (1130 feet per second at 70°F and sea level). That is, as wavelength increases, frequency decreases; or as frequency increases, wavelength decreases. Thus, for example, if frequency is increased from 1000 cps to 10,000 cps, and the velocity is 1130 feet per second, wave-length decreases from 1.130 feet to 0.1130 feet.

Sound intensity. Since sound is a form of energy and is considered relative to units of time, measurement of intensity fits the definition and units of measurement appropriate to *power.* The power transmitted per given area at right angle to the direction of sound wave travel is the wave *intensity.* The measurement units of intensity are watts[1] (power) per square centimeter (area). A sound that is just barely audible has an approximate intensity of:

$$\frac{1}{10,000,000,000,000,000}$$ watts per square centimeter. Obviously the above number even written in shorter form (10^{-16}) is inconvenient to handle. As we shall shortly describe, it becomes useful to incorporate intensity measures into a ratio called the *decibel* scale, and even to index intensity indirectly by actually measuring the acoustic pressure of sound waves.

Sound pressure. Like any pressure measure, acoustic pressure is measured in terms of force-per-unit-of-area. Typically, sound pressure, another amplitude measure is in terms of dynes[2] (force) per square centimeter (area). The necessary sound pressure for an audible sound seems almost nil. It is approximately 0.0002 dynes per square centimeter. Also like sound intensity, the decibel scale provides a more useful expression of measurement. In a general sense, sound intensity and pressure are different indexes of sound amplitude. It is usually easier to measure pressure than intensity.

Decibel scale. Our usual means for expressing intensity and sound pressure according to the decibel (dB) scale involves the definition of a ratio between some measured level and a reference level. But this ratio differs for the two qualities. A typical reference level for intensity is the barely audible level (10^{-16} watts per square centimeter). For sound pressure an analogous reference level is the pressure of a just audible sound (0.0002 dynes per square

---

[1] A *watt* (power unit) is 10,000,000 ergs (work unit) per second; an *erg* corresponds to the energy required by one dyne (force unit) to displace an object by one centimeter (distance unit); a *dyne* equals the force necessary to cause a mass of one gram to alter its speed by one centimeter per second for each second during which the force acts. As a power unit, one watt equals approximately $\frac{1}{746}$ horsepower.

[2] Dynes are defined in footnote 1.

centimeter). Because these ratios would involve unwieldy numbers and because we want to have dB references apply to corresponding intensity and pressure levels, we modify the above ratios somewhat. Sound intensity is 10 times the common log of an intensity ratio, and sound pressure is 20 times the common log of a pressure ratio.[3]

Speech in conversation averages about 60 dB in intensity or sound pressure relative to the above reference levels. For intensity this corresponds to an actual intensity which is 1,000,000 greater than the reference level (10^{-16} watts per centimeter squared). The common log of this ratio is 6; thus 10 times this common log, or 60, is the intensity in dB. The corresponding sound pressure ratio is an actual pressure that is 1000 greater than the reference level of 0.0002 dynes per centimeter squared. The common log of this ratio is 3; thus 20 times this common log, or 60, is the sound pressure in dB. Again, the ratios are defined so that they correspond to one another.

Psychological correlates. Thus far we have discussed sound in terms of its physical characteristics, that is, in terms of frequency and intensity of simple waves. The types of simple waves which we have described have psychological correlates often called *pure tones*. The variations which we perceive in pure tones and most sounds are psychological (or subjective) correlates of frequency and amplitude. Variations in frequency are perceived mainly as variations in the *pitch* of a sound, whereas variations in amplitude (intensity or pressure) are perceived mainly as variations in *loudness*. These correlations are the most exact when we are dealing with simple sound waves (i.e., pure tones).

Complex Waves

Periodic sounds. Nearly all of the sounds that we hear in everyday life, especially the sounds of speech, are not simple waves with pure tones but are mixtures of simple waves. These mixtures, or *complex waves*, are called *periodic* when they are combinations of wave forms that repeat themselves again and again. All periodic sounds can be described as the combination (or sum) of the simple sound waves which constitute them. Periodic waves are what we

[3] A common log is the power to which a base number of 10 must be raised to produce a given number. The common log of 100 is 2 (or 10^2); of 1,000 is 3 (10^3); or of 1,000,000 is 6 (10^6).

describe generally when we talk about speech sounds such as vowels, liquids (l, r), glides (w, y), and the nasals (m, n), that is, the *sonorant* speech sounds.

    Characteristics. Figure 2.4 illustrates the type of complex, or periodic, waveform that is produced when the vowel /a/ (as in "cot") is spoken and maintained. The dimensions of the waveform shown in figure 2.4 are the same as those which we have already discussed. The horizontal axis is time, and the vertical axis is amplitude. Note that the section of this wave labeled d is repeated

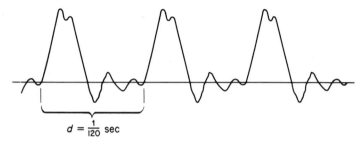

$$d = \tfrac{1}{120} \text{ sec}$$

Figure 2.4   The complex waveform of the vowel /a/ spoken and maintained.

in a cyclic fashion. Even though this is a complex wave it obeys all the relations of frequency, wavelength, and the velocity of sound which we have discussed so far.

    Again, all periodic sounds can be described as the combination or sum of simple sound waves. In figure 2.5, for example, the combination of the simple wave A (200 cps) with B (100 cps) is shown as complex wave C. When A and B are combined or summed their individual phases of compression and rarefaction will tend to reinforce or cancel each other with the result being a complex wave of the pattern shown in C. This summing can be done algebraically or graphically as shown in figure 2.5.

    Fundamental frequency. Since a complex periodic wave can be viewed as a portion of a waveform which keeps recurring, we can say that the frequency of the complex wave is the frequency at which this portion of the waveform keeps recurring. Thus, as illustrated in figures 2.4 and 2.5, the frequency of the complex waveform is the frequency at which the portion d keeps recurring. This frequency is called the *fundamental frequency* of the complex wave.

We can predict the fundamental frequency of complex wave C as shown in Figure 2.5. Assume, first, that at the beginning of each wave at t_0, waves A and B are starting their first cycle. At t_1, when wave A has finished its first cycle, wave B has finished only half of its first cycle. And at t_2 when wave A has finished its second cycle, wave B will just have completed its first cycle. Wave A begins its third cycle at the same time B begins its second one. Now consider the resultant curve C for the duration of t_0 and t_2. During

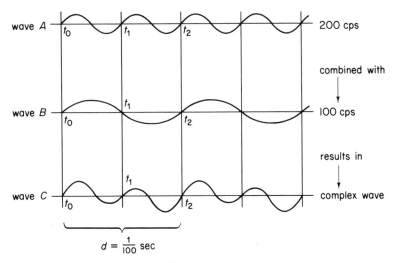

Figure 2.5   Simple wave combination.

the first two cycles of wave A, which was equivalent in time to the first cycle of wave B, we can see that the d portion of the resultant wave C would be produced. This would take $\frac{1}{100}$ second. At t_2 we are again at a point when both wave A and wave B are in the same configuration as they were at t_0. During the next $\frac{1}{100}$ second, we would expect things to proceed exactly as they did during the first $\frac{1}{100}$ second, and that the resultant complex wave C would consist of a pattern identical to that labeled as d. Since this identical pattern keeps recurring every $\frac{1}{100}$ second, the fundamental frequency of the resultant complex waveform is classified as 100 cps. That is, 100 times every second the configuration of the component waves (A and B) are back at the same beginning point as they were at t_0.

If we know the frequency of each of the simple wave components of a complex wave, we can find the fundamental frequency of the complex wave by determining the highest common denominator of the frequencies of its simple wave components. Thus, for example, 100 cps was the highest common denominator of 200 cps and 100 cps (Fig. 2.5).

Harmonics. A complex wave can have any number of simple wave components. Each such component of a periodic complex wave is called a *harmonic*. For purposes of discussion, table 2.1 summarizes the harmonics (*A–D*) and fundamental

	HARMONICS				
Sounds	*A*	*B*	*C*	*D*	*Fundamental*
i	500	700	1000	1400	100
ii	400	600	1200	1400	200
iii	300	900	1500	1800	300
iv	300	900	1500	1700	100

Table 2.1   The harmonics (*A . . . D*) and fundamental frequencies of four complex sounds (*i . . . iv*)

frequency of four complex sounds (*i–iv*). For each of these complex sounds *i* through *iv* the fundamental frequency can be obtained by finding the highest common denominator of the harmonics (*A* through *D*). For example, in complex wave *i*, 100 cps is the highest common denominator of 500, 700, 1000, and 1400 cps.

Figure 2.6 illustrates an analysis of the simple wave components of complex wave *iv* from table 2.1. One point in this illustration is that the harmonics of the complex wave do not each have the same amplitude. If we assume that simple wave *D* has an amplitude of one, we can see that, relatively speaking, wave *A* has an amplitude of only one-third of this, wave *B* an amplitude of twice this, and wave *C* an amplitude of only half of this reference amplitude.

In voiced speech sounds, the harmonics are simple waves evenly spaced across frequencies, and the fundamental frequency of the resultant complex wave equals the frequency of the lowest simple wave frequency (called the *first harmonic*). For example, if we speak with a fundamental frequency of 120 cps, the first harmonic will have a frequency of 120 cps, the second harmonic will have a frequency of 240 cps, the third 360 cps, and so on.

Spectrum. The types of characteristics which we have been discussing, together define what we call the *spectral* characteristics of sound, or as applied to speech, the *spectrum* of a speech wave. These characteristics include frequency and amplitude of the

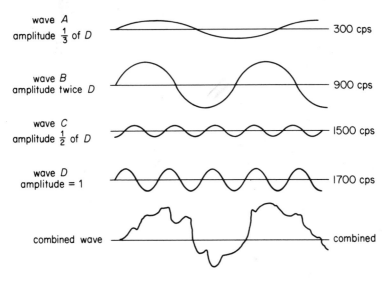

Figure 2.6   Graphic analysis of wave *iv* from Table 2.1.

simple wave components, and their combination as complex waves. The regularities of such combinations can be analyzed and described mathematically by what is called *Fourier analysis*. The graphic portrayal of complex waves can take a number of forms. For example, figure 2.7 illustrates a relatively simple graphic portrayal of all the main information that we might typically be interested in when portraying the characteristics of the complex wave illustrated in figure 2.6. In figure 2.7 on the horizontal axis we plot the frequency of the simple wave components of the complex wave, and on the vertical axis we plot the amplitude of each of these simple wave components.

Often in the analysis and display of speech sounds an instrument called the *sound spectrograph* is employed. Some of the graphic displays, or *spectrograms,* produced by a spectrograph are shown in figure 2.8. In example 2.8a, time is represented from left to right along the horizontal axis; frequency is represented on the vertical axis, and intensity (amplitude) of the signal is represented by the darkness of the tracings. In essence, a spectrogram plots the concentrations of energies in the frequency spectrum of a complex sound, and gives a picture of this across a period of time. A spectrogram shown in figure 2.8b represents another type of display, this one portraying amplitude along the vertical axis and

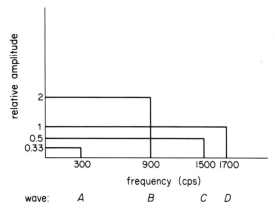

Figure 2.7 Graphic portrayal of amplitude-by-frequency of the complex wave shown in figure 2.6.

frequency along the horizontal axis. This latter display more or less represents a section taken out of the speech wave, where intensity, rather than being represented by darkness of the tracings, is assigned to a coordinate in the display. Spectrograms, then, provide us with the means to simultaneously display the key characteristics of a sound spectrum, that is, frequency, amplitude, and time.

Aperiodic waves. Not all complex sounds have simple wave components that are multiples of some fundamental frequency. Such sounds which may have components at any or all frequencies are called *aperiodic waves.* This is the chief acoustic characteristic that separates sounds from what we typically call *noises.* Speech sounds such as z, s, d, t, v, f, b, p, or *obstruents,* are comprised in part of aperiodic noises. Figure 2.9 illustrates by use of spectrograms the contrast between the spectral characteristics of periodic

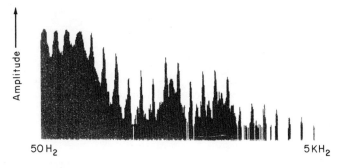

Frequency, 50 to 5,000 H_2

(b)

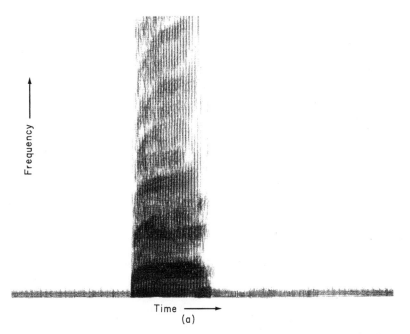

Time ⟶

(a)

Figure 2.8 Spectrographic displays (a) frequency by time, (b) amplitude by frequency.

17

and aperiodic sounds involved in speech. The spectrogram in figure 2.9a is the vowel /a/ in English, whereas figure 2.9b is the /š/ sound of English. Note in figure 2.9a how the harmonics and fundamental frequency are easily identifiable in the spectral pattern,

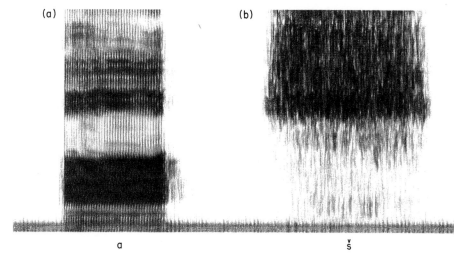

(a)   (b)

a   š

Figure 2.9   Spectral qualities of [a] and [š] sounds.

whereas in figure 2.9b the acoustic energy has a more random distribution across part of the frequency spectrum.

Resonance

As we have just seen, speech sounds are complex waves, and their acoustic characteristics, particularly of sonorants (vowels, liquids, glides, nasals), involve harmonic patterns. A thorough understanding of the nature of speech sounds requires some knowledge of how such patterns are generally produced. Much of this knowledge requires an understanding of an acoustic phenomenon called *resonance*—that is, how the acoustic pattern of sound is modified by an enclosure. In speech, this enclosure comprises the oral and pharyngeal (throat) cavities, and for some sounds, the nasal cavities. The spectral patterns of *sonorant* speech sounds can be explained by the controllable resonance characteristics of these cavities. In particular, it is useful for us to consider the resonance qualities of tubes, since the vocal tract has tube-like resonance qualities.

Wave Reflection

As an introduction to the concept of resonance, we will consider how sound waves are reflected by surfaces, and then how reflected waves may interfere with incoming waves so as to diminish

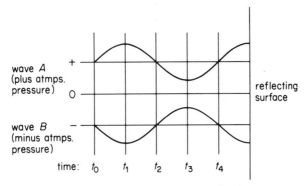

Figure 2.10   Example of wave reflection.

or reinforce them. Imagine, for example, how the vibrating molecules which comprise sound waves strike a rigid wall, for instance. When this happens, the molecules exert a force against this wall, and the wall (theoretically) exerts an equal force in the opposite direction. Recall that we characterize sound as periodic variations in air pressure. This means that, if air in the vicinity of the wall is subjected to a periodic acoustic disturbance, the air pressure at the wall will vary periodically. Figure 2.10 summarizes the way in which the force exerted against the wall of a given area would fluctuate in the presence of a 500 cps tone produced by a tuning fork. It would fluctuate around the atmospheric pressure ("0" in Fig. 2.10) such that it would be slightly more than atmospheric

pressure when a wave crest (compression phase) from the tuning
fork hits the wall, and slightly below atmospheric pressure when a
wave trough (rarefaction) arrives at the wall. Wave A in figure
2.10 represents the force exerted on the wall by a sound wave
emanating from the tuning fork as a function of time $(t_0 \ldots t_4)$.
The wave B, representing the wall forces, also fluctuates around a
quantity equal to atmospheric pressure, but radiates in the opposite
direction. That is why its baseline is labelled minus atmospheric
pressure. In this figure, we consider a force directed to the right
to be a positive force, and a force directed to the left to be a negative
one.

Consider what happens when a crest from the tuning fork
(curve A) arrives at the wall at t_1. More pressure is exerted against
the wall than at t_0, when the positive pressure equalled positive
atmospheric pressure. Therefore, in order to counteract this increase in pressure, the wall must exert more force (curve B) against
the air, but in the opposite (negative) direction. Thus, as diagrammed
in figure 2.10, whenever a crest of the original wave arrives at the
wall, the wall produces a trough. Similarly, a trough in the original
wave causes the wall to produce a crest. Similar generalizations
can be made for any other instant of time depicted in figure 2.10.
The point is that the force exerted by the wall is varying periodically, and its frequency is the same as that of the sound. Since we
consider any object which exerts a periodically varying pressure
against the air to be a sound source, we can consider the wall itself
a sound source. This source always has the same frequency as the
sound in the adjacent medium, but—and this is the crucial point—
the wall sound source always acts so as to exactly counteract the
fluctuating air pressure at the wall. The wave motion produced by
the wall is called the *reflected wave*.

Cancellation in Tube Resonance

If the wall in the above example were located at the
closed end of a tube and the sound source were at the open end, we
would have a situation where originating and returning (reflected)
waves interfered with one another. If the returning wave is exactly
the opposite of the originating wave, the effect is one of cancellation.

For example, suppose, as shown in figure 2.11 that a tuning
fork produces a 500 cps tone at the open end of a tube which is

68.8 cm, or one wavelength, long. At a given time, as shown in curve *A*, when the fork is creating a crest, there is a crest at the closed end of the tube because it is exactly one wavelength away. Simultaneously, the wall is producing its trough, as shown in curve *B*. This means, too, that there is a trough one wavelength from the wall to the fork. The trough caused by the reflected wave cancels the crest of the fork-caused wave.

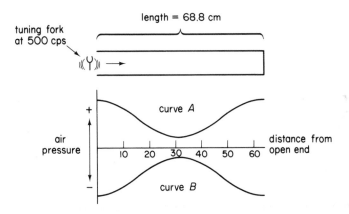

Figure 2.11   Example of wave cancellation.

Cancellation will also take place if the tube is exactly one-half the wavelength. This can also be visualized in figure 2.11; just imagine that the closed end of the tube is located 34.4 cm from the fork, where a trough of the fork-producing wave (*A*) corresponds to a crest in the wall-reflecting wave (*B*).

We can generalize from the above that if the length of the tube is $\frac{1}{2}$, 1, $1\frac{1}{2}$, 2, $2\frac{1}{2}$, etc. times the wavelength, cancellation will take place.

Reinforcement in Tube Resonance

Tubes closed at one end can also cause reflected waves to reinforce originating waves. This will occur, for example, when a tube length is three-fourths a wavelength. Consider figure 2.12 where a 500 cps sound source is at the open end of a tube 51.6 cm long. At three-fourths of the wavelength of the originating wave (*A*), the wall would be at the midpoint between a trough and crest.

A quarter of a second before this time, the wall had experienced a crest. The reflected wave (*B*), therefore, is also at this midpoint, but a quarter of a second earlier it had been a trough. Relative to the open end of the tube, the reflected wave is a trough, but so is the originating wave. (The total distance from the fork to the wall and back to the fork is one and one-half wavelengths, or from a crest through another crest to a trough.) Returning and originating waves thus reinforce one another. Reinforcement also occurs when

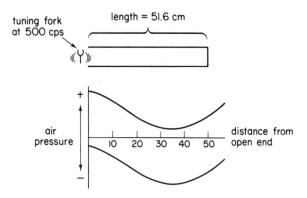

Figure 2.12   Example of wave reinforcement.

the tube length is one-fourth the wavelength. In fact, we can generalize that reinforcement will occur when the length of the tube is $\frac{1}{4}$, $\frac{3}{4}$, $1\frac{1}{4}$, $1\frac{3}{4}$, etc. the wavelength.

Further Resonance Characteristics of Tubes

Modes.   As we have seen, a tube of length *l* will reinforce any tone which has a wavelength *L* when *l* is $\frac{1}{4}$, $\frac{3}{4}$, $\frac{5}{4}$, etc. times *L*. The term *mode* is frequently used to refer to the frequencies which are reinforced by a resonating system such as the tube. The frequency which has a wavelength four times the length of the tube closed at one end is called the *first mode;* the frequency with a wavelength four-thirds the length of the tube is the *second mode;* and so on.

The cancelled frequencies will be those which have a wavelength which is twice the length of the tube, equal to the length of the tube, two-thirds the length of the tube, and so on. These are

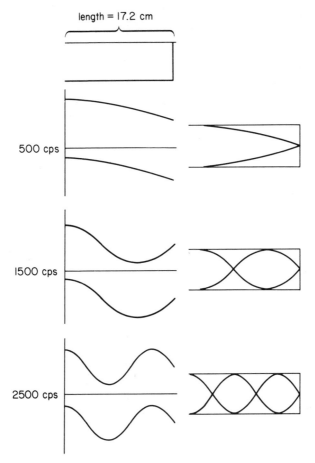

Figure 2.13   Examples of tube resonance modes.

sometimes referred to as the *anti-resonances*. However, we will focus our attention for now only on the resonances, or modes.

Consider a tube 17.2 cm in length. Since the wavelength of a 500 cps tone is four times the length of the tube, 500 cps is the first mode of this tube; 1500 cps is the second mode; 2500 is the third mode, and so on. The first three modes of such a tube are represented in figure 2.13.

Nodes and loops.   Observe an interesting property of each mode: The first mode has one point where the original wave and the reflected wave always cancel—at the wall—and one point where the two waves always reinforce each other—at the open end. Let us refer to a point of cancellation as a *node* and to a point where reinforcement takes place as a *loop*. Now notice that the second mode has two nodes and two loops. The third mode has three of each, and so on.

  Complex sounds. As we have already said, given the characteristics of a closed-end tube we can anticipate what frequencies

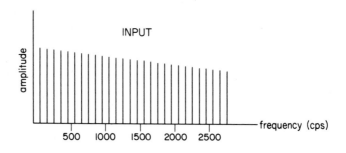

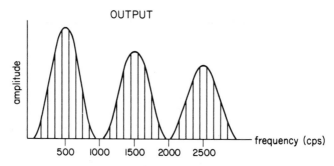

Figure 2.14 Example of tube resonance characteristics.

it will reinforce. Accordingly, we would expect that a complex sound which contains components at these frequencies would have these components reinforced by the tube. Consider figure 2.14. Here we have a tube 17.2 cm long and a complex tone with a fundamental frequency of 100 cps. The wavelengths of, for example, the 500 cps, the 1500 cps, and the 2500 cps components of the complex wave are, respectively, 68.8 cm, 22.9 cm, 13.8 cm. These components will resonate since they are, respectively, 4, $\frac{4}{3}$, and $\frac{4}{5}$

times the length of the tube; in other words, these components constitute the first three modes of the tube. Thus, if this complex tone were to be the input into the tube, the output might be as depicted in figure 2.14.

Formants. Notice that in figure 2.14 the outputs that show reinforcement incorporate *bands of frequencies*. These reinforced frequency bands are called *formants*. Formants are formed when a tube's resonance qualities reinforce frequencies close to the resonant frequencies as well as the resonant frequencies themselves. As can be seen in figure 2.14, these additional reinforcements are less as they deviate from the main resonant frequencies. The prediction of how much reinforcement will take place a given interval away from the resonant frequency can only be answered by a further study of such properties of the tube as its diameter and the properties of the material out of which the tube is made.

Tube Resonance in Speech

It has been known for over one hundred years that we recognize vowels by virtue of their frequencies. Associated with each vowel is a unique configuration of the tongue, jaw, lips, and velum (soft palate) which determines the mode-frequencies of the vocal tract. No matter what the fundamental frequency of vocal sound production (used as the example of input tone in Fig. 2.14), the formant frequencies will be the same for a given set of positions of the articulating organs. It is these formant frequencies which provide the perceptual clues necessary for determining the vowel.

Of course, the vocal tract is not exactly a closed-end straight-wall tube, such as we have been discussing. For one thing, if we consider the vocal folds to be the closed end, then we see that the sound input seems to be from the closed end, rather than the open end. However, this does not cause any difficulties. Even if we were to consider the input to the tube examples discussed so far to be through a small opening in the closed end of the tube, we would find that the mode frequencies remain unchanged. The major difference between the tubes we have been discussing and the vocal tract is that the vocal tract deviates from the straight-walled tubes in that there are constrictions located at various points in the tube. These enter into the production of speech sounds as discussed in Chapter 3.

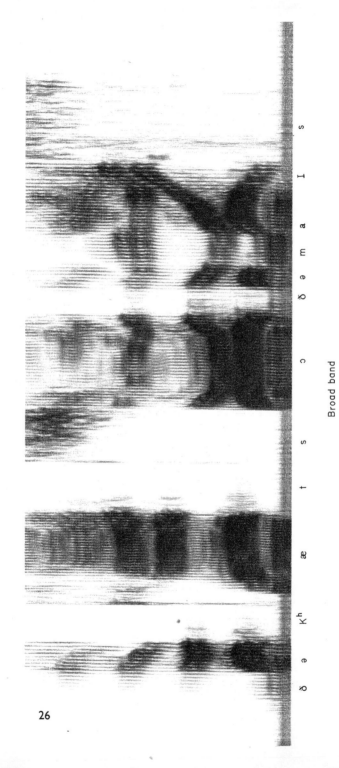

Broad band

Figure 2.15   Spectrogram of continuous speech.

26

The Speech Spectrum

In the simplest view, the speech spectrum is made up of harmonic patterns for vowels, noise patterns for consonants, and primarily the way these patterns vary dynamically across time. Again, the sound spectrograph provides an excellent means of illustration for us. Figure 2.15 is a spectrogram of the English sentence, "The cats saw the mice." This is a broad band spectrogram which shows the time sequence more accurately than harmonics. However, we can interpret this sequence in terms of what it signifies of the relation between the acoustics and articulation of speech.

Each vertical striation (narrow band) on the spectrogram corresponds to a glottal pulse—the brief period of time when the glottis is open and air flows through. Between these striations, the glottis is momentarily closed and no acoustic energy is produced. Let us examine the broad band spectrogram closely and correlate aspects of the sound with what we can infer about the articulatory activity which produces this utterance. The first phonetic symbol, [ð], is a low energy, voiced sound and is followed by the vowel, [ə]. Notice that the transition from the consonant to the vowel is rather abrupt. This corresponds to the moment that the tongue is withdrawn from the interdental position and is quickly placed in the position for [ə]. When the tongue is in the vocalic position, there is less acoustic resistance and a louder sound can be produced. This vowel is then followed by the voiceless stop, [k]. There is. a moment of silence during this stop followed by a burst of air upon the release of the stop. This is written phonetically with a small [ʰ], indicating aspiration. It shows up as a short period of high frequency, rather incomplete, striations. These striations are not regularly spaced, like the ones indicating glottal pulses. This shows that this period is not a voiced sound, but rather white noise (a mixture of multiple frequencies). The period of aspiration is then followed by the vowel [æ], where the formants are clearly distinguishable. Following the vowel, again we have a voiceless stop, [t], which is followed by an [s]. The [s] shows up as a period of high frequency white noise. The vowel [ɔ] shows some particularly interesting properties. As the tongue moves from the high front position for the production of [s] to the low back position for [ɔ], it must, of course, go through a range of intermediate positions. During this time, sound is still being produced at the glottis. Therefore it is to be expected that during the transition period changing formants should be seen in the spectrogram. Notice that the first formant rises from a low position—corresponding to closure at the alveolar ridge; and the second formant falls—corresponding to a constriction about a third of the way in from the lips, at the gum ridge—during the transition from the [s] to the [ɔ]. Similar transitions—only in reverse, so to speak—can be seen in the transition from [ɔ] to [ð], at the end of the vowel. Notice that the [m] in the word "mice" shows up as a low energy, voiced segment with formant frequencies of its own corresponding to the resonant properties of the nasal cavities. The formant transitions as the tongue produces the [aɪ] diphthong in the word "mice" are quite striking. For the low, back unrounded vowel [a], there is a high first formant and a low second formant. In fact, these two formants are very close to each other here. However, for the high, front, unrounded vowel [i], the first formant is low and the second formant is high. This spectrogram illustrates the behavior of these formants in the [aɪ] diphthong very clearly. The final [s] shows up, again, as high frequency noise, only longer and weaker than the [s] in "saw."

3 Phonological Perspectives[1]

As we saw in Chapter 2, it is possible to talk about the sounds of speech in terms of their acoustic characteristics. Such characteristics enable us to identify the physical properties of speech, as well as indicating the general nature of man's capabilities for speech production. In this chapter we turn from the discussion of the acoustic aspects of speech to a consideration of how speech sounds serve as units of linguistic structure. The study of linguistically significant aspects of speech sounds is known as *phonology*. *Physical phonetics*, which has been illustrated in the previous chapter, is more concerned with physical properties of speech sounds, irrespective of the phonological role they may play.

It is important to distinguish between *systematic* phonetics, which is a part of phonology, and physical phonetics, which belongs more properly to physics. A systematic phonetic representation of an utterance will involve all the information which is relevant to the sound pattern of a language, but will ignore many physical characteristics of speech sounds themselves. For example, a systematic phonetic representation of an utterance will not record whether a sound was spoken by a young or old speaker, a man or a woman, or by someone who has a bad cold. These factors play no role in the phonological system of a language, although they do play a role in determining the physical shape of speech sounds. The symbols used in systematic phonetics are shown in table 3.1.

[1] Charles Cairns, Queens College, is coauthor of this chapter.

29

A phonemic representation will use, by and large, the same system of symbols as the systematic phonetic representation.[2] The main differences between these two levels of phonology lies in the fact that phonemic representations have been defined as those sound segments which provide for minimum distinctions in expression (e.g., "bat-pat") in a given language that are also minimum distinctions in meaning, whereas phonetic representations are written symbols for speech sounds.

Current phonological theory, however, holds that the basic sound distinctions of language are not sound segments themselves, but are the phonetic features which distinguish such segments, as in how voicing distinguishes between /b/ and /p/. Accordingly, sound segments are best defined as "bundles" of phonetic features, and those features which provide the minimum contrast between segments are known as *distinctive* features. The concept of distinctive features, the main topic of this chapter, serves as an introduction to one level of linguistic study. This introduction is presented along with brief discussions of the production and reception aspects of speech.

The Production Apparatus

System Subdivisions

Many approaches to the physiology of speech production encompass a description of the three main subdivisions shown in figure 3.1. These include the *respiratory* system, which provides the movement of air for speech; the *laryngeal* system, which includes among other things the vocal folds which serve in the transduction of moving air into acoustic energy (*phonation*); and the *supraglottal* system which incorporates the oral and nasal cavities, the tongue, lips, and jaw.

---

[2] By convention, systematic phonetic symbols are often enclosed in brackets while phonemes, which use mostly the same symbols, are enclosed between slashes. Thus [s] refers to a specific sound, but /s/ to a basic sound category of which [s] would be one way of saying a sound of that category. In this text, brackets and slashes are only used where their absence would result in ambiguity.

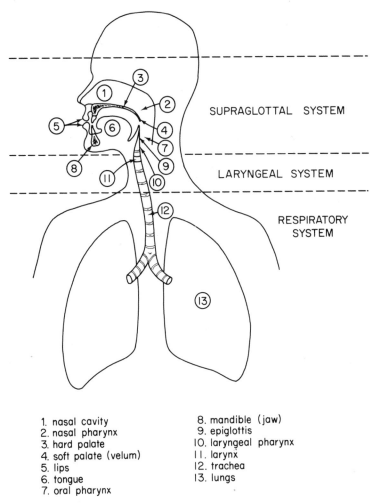

1. nasal cavity
2. nasal pharynx
3. hard palate
4. soft palate (velum)
5. lips
6. tongue
7. oral pharynx

8. mandible (jaw)
9. epiglottis
10. laryngeal pharynx
11. larynx
12. trachea
13. lungs

Figure 3.1   The production apparatus.

Such subdivisions of the speech apparatus can easily lead to the oversimplified belief that speech physiology is a simple three-part system. On the contrary, speech production is perhaps the most all-encompassing, complex neuro-muscular activity of the human organism. It involves coordination of nerves and muscle from the waist up, and the almost incredibly intricate coordination of the fast-moving oral articulators.

Articulators.

We will examine the several aspects of speech physiology necessary for a basic discussion of the sounds of speech. These aspects are illustrated in more detail in figure 3.2. (Note the correspondence between the numbers in figure 3.2 and the following paragraphs.)

1. *Larynx.* The larynx is the so-called voice box; it houses the vocal folds which serve as a sound source (phonation) for speech. You can easily detect the difference between voiced and unvoiced speech sounds by switching between the articulation of *s* ("*s*ill") and *z* ("*z*eal"). The voicing associated with *z* appears as a very audible buzz, which can be heard if you put your fingers in your ears while producing it. Compare this with *s* which is unvoiced. Note particularly that this voicing is the only feature that differentiates these two sounds.

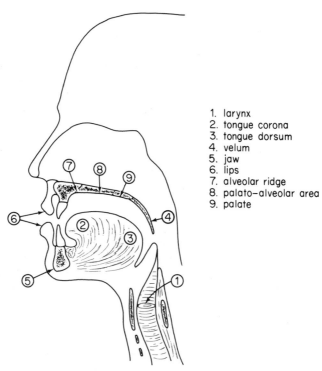

1. larynx
2. tongue corona
3. tongue dorsum
4. velum
5. jaw
6. lips
7. alveolar ridge
8. palato–alveolar area
9. palate

Figure 3.2   The supraglottal system.

2. *Tongue corona.* The coronal area is the tip and forward edge (or blade) of the tongue. You can detect the action of the corona by producing such sounds as *t* ("*t*ill"), *d* ("*d*ill"), *s* ("*s*il"), *z* ("*z*eal"), or *n* ("*n*il"). Note how, for these sounds, the corona contacts the alveolar ridge—that is, the hard ridge of tissue immediately behind the front, upper teeth.

The production of *t* and *d* involves a complete closure (*stop*) between the tongue and the alveolar ridge, which halts the air flow. By contrast, for the sounds *s* and *z* a long, narrow groove is formed along the center of the tongue. Except for this groove, the tongue is pressed tightly against the alveolar ridge. As air is forced through this groove and strikes the back of the front teeth, a hissing (*fricative*) sound is made.

The corona is inserted between the teeth for the sounds θ ("*th*ink") and ð ("*th*y"). Note again that a fricative sound is produced, but because the constriction is not as narrow as with *s* and *z* and because the air does not hit a further obstruction (such as the back of the teeth), θ and ð are not as noisy.

The corona can also be brought in contact with the palatal or palato-alveolar areas. English does not have any palatal sounds, although it is common in Spanish (ñ, "mañana"). The sounds *č* ("*ch*urch"), *ǰ* ("*j*udge"), *š* ("*sh*ell"), and *ž* ("a*z*ure") are palato-alveolar consonants in English. Note how *č* and *ǰ* involve more complex articulatory gestures than do *š* and *ž*. The former are produced by first forming a complete closure between the tongue and the roof of the mouth. The closure is slowly released with the central portion of the tongue opening first. This creates a narrow opening which acts as a noise source for a very brief time until the tongue is withdrawn so that the air can flow past without obstruction. These sounds are called *affricates*.

3. *Tongue dorsum.* Note how the sounds *k* ("*k*ill") and *g* ("*g*ill") involve bringing the rear of the tongue body (or dorsum) into contact with the palate. These are consonant sounds which require a tongue movement, but use the entire tongue body rather than just the corona.

4. *Velum.* The velum is a valve which can open to allow the air stream to pass through the nasal passageway. It is closed for most speech sounds, although in restful breathing it usually hangs open. Nasal consonant sounds such as *n* ("*n*il") and *m* ("*m*ill") involve an open velum. In the production of these sounds

all of the air flowing out of the lungs moves through the nasal passageway. Vowels may have a nasal quality; this is common in French. In English, vowels sometimes become nasalized when they precede a nasal consonant (as in "can't"); here the air stream is split into both the oral and nasal cavities.

    5. *Jaw.* The jaw position is the main determinant of tongue height in vowel production. Note the different jaw positions for the articulation of *a* ("c*a*lm") and Ω("b*oo*k"), or the difference within the diphthongs *a*ʊ ("out") and *e*ɪ ("d*a*te").

    6. *Lips.* In the sounds *p* ("*p*ill") and *b* ("*b*ill"), the lips are completely closed and block the flow of air; these are called *bilabial stops.* By contrast, note how the sounds *f* ("*f*ill") and *v* ("*v*ow") are produced with the lower lip pressed against the upper teeth (*labiodental*), creating a narrow air passageway and a friction-like noise (*fricative*). In vowel or semivowel sounds such as *u* ("r*u*le") and *w* ("wow"), the lips are protruded and brought into proximity to one another, creating a rounding effect. In sounds such as *i* ("b*ee*t"), *e* ("b*e*t"), or æ ("b*a*t") the lips are spread apart.

Classification by Distinctive Features

The Concept of Distinctive Features

    From the preceding discussion, it should seem reasonable to you that speech sounds could be classified in terms of their articulatory characteristics. For many years it has been traditional to talk about vowels in terms of tongue position and height, and consonants in terms of the articulators and type of sound (or "place" and "manner") involved in production. In recent years, phonological theory has moved to a system of distinctive feature classification based upon articulatory contrasts among phonetic segments. Here the aim has been to identify a system which differentiates every sound segment from every other segment by a phonetic or distinctive feature. Relative to phonological theory, it is intended that this system be universal to the languages of the world. It is most important to note that distinctive features systems are not intended as refinements in the descriptions of articulation already available from research in acoustic and physiological phonetics. Instead they are intended as the most economical description of phonemic (rather than phonetic) contrasts, and as such, may differ in some cases from the details of the phonetician's description of articulation. We should note, too, that distinctive features descriptions are still subject to refinement relative to advances in phonological theory.

The distinctive features approach is important to us for several reasons. One is that the contemporary research literature in phonology often uses distinctive feature classifications; hence, knowing them will aid you in further study. Another reason is that the distinctive features approach is incorporated into the framework of *generative grammar*, a theoretical approach in linguistics to be discussed in the next chapter. Finally, the theory of distinctive features has played an important role in the development of several contemporary models of speech production.

The major classifications of sounds in terms of distinctive features dates back to Jakobson (1941), and a more recent system is presented by Chomsky and Halle (1968). The scheme to be discussed is a slight modification of the latter system. It differs in detail rather than concept, however.

Feature Specification

Table 3.1 presents a distinctive feature matrix of English sounds. For each sound at the top of a column in this matrix, the entries in the row indicate the presence $(+)$, absence $(-)$, or irrelevance (no entry) of an articulatory feature.

There are several general characteristics to be noted in table 3.1. Most important is that every sound differs from every other sound by at least one feature. Second, the sounds are divided into groups. For example, the usual gross distinction between consonants (obstructed air passage in the vocal tract) and vowels (relatively unobstructed air passage) can be seen in the differentiation between sounds classified as *consonantal* $(+$ in top row) and *nonconsonantal* $(-)$. Finally, the sounds of most languages can be specified within the chart shown in table 3.1.

The key to using the distinctive feature system is, of course, to know definitions of the distinctions labeled in the left column of table 3.1. We will briefly summarize them.

Consonantal. Essentially, sounds classed as consonantal require that there be a constriction somewhere along the center

Table 3.1 — Distinctive features of English phonemes

	l	r	n	m	ŋ	z	s	ð	θ	d	t	v	f	b	p	ž	š	ǰ	č	g	k	u	ɔ	a	o	i	æ	e	w	y	h
consonantal	+	+	+	+	+	+	+	+	+	+	+	+	+	+	+	+	+	+	+	+	+	−	−	−	−	−	−	−	−	−	−
vocalic	+	+	−	−	−	−	−	−	−	−	−	−	−	−	−	−	−	−	−	−	−	+	+	+	+	+	+	+	−	−	−
nasal	−	−	+	+	+	−	−	−	−	−	−	−	−	−	−	−	−	−	−	−	−										
lateral	+	−	−	−	−	−	−	−	−	−	−	−	−	−	−	−	−	−	−	−	−										
anterior	+	+	+	+	−	+	+	+	+	+	+	+	+	+	+	−	−	−	−	−	−										
coronal	+	+	+	−	−	+	+	+	+	+	+	−	−	−	−	+	+	+	+	−	−										
continuant	+	+	−	−	−	+	+	+	+	−	−	+	+	−	−	+	+	−	−	−	−										
strident	−	−	−	−	−	+	+	−	−	−	−	+	+	−	−	+	+	+	+	−	−										
voice	+	+	+	+	+	+	−	+	−	+	−	+	−	+	−	+	−	+	−	+	−										
back																						+	+	+	+	−	−	−	+	−	
high																						+	−	−	−	+	−	−	+	+	
low																						−	+	+	−	−	+	−	−	−	
round																						+	+	−	+	−	−	−	+	−	
del. release										−	−			−	−			+	+	−	−										

Consonants:
/l/ fill
/r/ rill
/n/ nil
/m/ mill
/ŋ/ tang
/z/ zeal
/s/ sill
/ð/ thy

/θ/ thigh
/d/ drill
/t/ till
/v/ ville
/f/ fill
/b/ bill
/p/ pill
/ž/, /ʒ/[1] rouge

/š/, /ʃ/[1] shall
/ǰ/, /dʒ/[1] Jill
/č/, /tʃ/[1] chill
/g/ gill
/k/ kill

Vowels and glides:[2]
/u/ boot   /w/ will
/ɔ/ saw   /y/ yet
/a/ cot   /h/ hoe
/o/ boat
/i/ beet
/æ/ bat
/e/ bait

Table 3.1   Distinctive features of English phonemes

[1] Alternative symbols are given.

[2] The simplified system portrayed here is meant to illustrate the application of the feature concept to vowels in general rather than a complete description of the vowel system of English. English also contains a distinction between tense and lax vowels such as the vowels in "bait" [bet] and "bet" [bɛt]. Moreover, there are several different phonetically occurring vowels, such as the vowels in the words "cut" [kʌt], "bird" [bɔd], "sofa" [sofə]. Students who wish to see the feature system applied in detail should consult Chomsky and Halle (1968).

line of the oral cavity, and for some sounds this may be accompanied by further constrictions. The constriction may be at the lips *b*, *p*, *m*; tongue and teeth θ, ð; teeth and lip *f*, *v*; tongue and alveolar or palatal area *d*, *t*, *z*, *s*, *ǰ*, *č*, *ž*, *š*; or tongue and velar area *g*, *k*, *ŋ*, to mention most consonantal sounds. The sounds *r* and *l* involve a sufficiently narrow constriction at the center line to be classed as consonantal, although they are relatively open at the sides. The vowels and glides (i.e., *w*, *y*, *h*) are, by contrast, classed as nonconsonantal.

Vocalic. Sounds having relatively little or no obstruction in the oral cavity, as measured in terms of the total cross-sectional area of the point of maximum constriction, are vocalic. Obviously, all of the vowels are vocalic. But not all vocalic sounds are vowels. The liquids *l* and *r*, although having a centrally located constriction, are sufficiently unobstructed around the sides of the constriction to be classed as vocalic. The glides *w*, *y*, *h*, mark a dividing line of sounds that are obstructed enough to be nonvocalic, but the center line constriction is not narrow enough to class them as consonantal.

Note that in terms of the above two distinctive features, all of the sounds in table 3.1 can be grouped into four categories:

		Features	
Category	*Examples*	consonantal	vocalic
consonants	*n . . . k*	+	−
vowels	*u . . . e*	−	+
liquids	*l, r*	+	+
glides	*w, y, h*	−	−

Nasal. In articulatory terms, nasals are characterized by lowering of the velum (Fig. 3.2) which opens the nasal cavity for sound resonation. As can be seen in table 3.1, the nasal feature distinguishes *m*, *n*, and *ŋ* from the other consonants. In fact, addition of this feature to the scheme provides for the differentiation of all the speech sounds into the categories of *sonorants* and *obstruents*. Sonorants include glides, liquids, vowels, and nasals. All the remaining consonants are obstruents. The meaning of the obstruent label becomes clear when it is realized that these are the only sound for which the air stream is forced to overcome an obstruction in the passage from the lungs to the outside of the body. There is no such obstruction for the nasals, since the air stream is relatively

unimpeded in its passage through the nasal cavities. (Nasal consonants are still classified as consonantal and nonvocalic, however,
because these features are defined on the positions of the organs in
the oral cavity, regardless of the state of the velum.) The liquids
allow sufficient area around the sides of the constriction located at
the center of the oral cavity to be classified as sonorants. Obviously,
there is no significant obstruction in the case of the vowels.

Coronal. The articulation of some sounds directly involves
the corona, or front part of the tongue. For example, obstruents
z, *s*, *d*, and *t* are coronal whereas the obstruents *v*, *f*, *b*, *k*, *g*, and *p*
are noncoronal.

Continuant. If the obstruction in the oral cavity (only) does
not completely block the flow of air, the sound is classed as continuant—as, for example, in the distinction between θ (continuant)
and *t* (noncontinuant). All vowels are, of course, continuants, and
so are glides and liquids because of the continuous flow of air through
the mouth. Among the consonants, the continuants are the fricative
sounds (i.e., *v*, *f*, θ, ð, *s*, *z*, *š*, *ž*). The only noncontinuant consonants are the oral stops *b*, *p*, *d*, *t*, *g*, *k*, and the affricatives *č* and
ǐ (even though they involve a continuant portion), and nasals *m*, *n*, ŋ.

Voice. Sounds classified as voiced incorporate vocal fold
phonation in their articulation, as in the production of all vowels,
liquids, glides, and nasals. Obstruents such as *z* and *s*, *d* and *t*,
v and *f*, and *b* and *p*, are differentiated in terms of being voiced and
unvoiced respectively. In fact, we can completely differentiate
among these obstruents in terms of the features of coronal, continuant, and voice.

| | *Features* | | |
Sound	coronal	continuant	voice
z	+	+	+
s	+	+	−
d	+	−	+
t	+	−	−
v	−	+	+
f	−	+	−
b	−	−	+
p	−	−	−

Anterior. If the point of articulation is as far front in the
oral cavity as the alveolar ridge (Fig. 3.2) or farther, the sound has

the feature · of anterior; if not that far front, it is nonanterior. Thus, for example, *p* and *t* are anterior, whereas *č* and *k* are nonanterior.

Strident. A strident sound is produced by an obstruction in the oral cavity which forces the air through a relatively long, narrow constriction. As the air rushes out of the opening of this constriction, its turbulence serves as a primary noise source; this turbulent air is then directed against a second obstruction which causes a secondary noise source. For example, *s* and *z* are strident, but ð and θ are nonstrident because they lack secondary noise characteristics.

Note below how the strident feature differentiates among selected obstruents:

| | *Features* | | |
Sound	continuant	voice	strident
z	+	+	+
s	+	−	+
ð	+	+	−
θ	+	−	−

Delayed release. Recall that affricates are oral stops (i.e., noncontinuant obstruents) for which the articulators are released in such a way as to provide for a brief period during the release when the articulators form a narrow passageway for the production of a fricative portion of the sound. Affricates are classified as having this feature of delayed release, as contrasted with all other oral stops. This feature is not defined for continuants. Also, it is not possible for a nasal sound to be an affricate, because there must be a build up of air pressure behind the obstruction during the completely blocked portion of the sound for the production of friction during the release gesture. This is impossible for the nasals, since air is allowed to escape through the nasal passageways. The sounds ĵ and *č* are the only affricates in English.

It is interesting to note that the feature of delayed release is not necessary for the most economical differentiation of English speech sounds. That is, it is not necessary to refer to this feature when specifying the minimum number of features necessary for keeping each English sound distinct from all the other sounds.

This is so because the only affricates in English are also the only palato-alveolar stops; thus č and ǰ can be completely distinguished from the other noncontinuant sounds by the coronal and nonanterior features.

Lateral. A lateral sound is one which involves a contact between the corona of the tongue and some point of the roof of the mouth, along with a simultaneous lowering of the sides of the

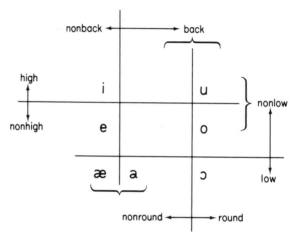

Figure 3.3   The vowel distinctions.

tongue. In English, *l* is a lateral sound, and this feature differentiates it from *r* the only other glide, which is nonlateral.

At this point we have described sufficient features to differentiate all of the consonantal sounds of English. (You may wish to refer to table 3.1 to check on this.) We turn next to those features which enable the differentiation of vowels.

High. Figure 3.3 shows a simplified version of the English vowel system. The vowels which involve the highest tongue position—that is, the narrowest constriction in the oral cavity for vowel production—are at the top of the figure. These vowels, *u* and *i*, have the feature *high;* all others are nonhigh.

Low. The vowels *æ*, *a*, and *ɔ* involve the lowest tongue position. As shown in figure 3.3, these vowels have the feature *low;*

all other vowels are nonlow. Note how the so-called middle height vowels are classed in this system; *e* and *o* are nonlow and nonhigh.

Back. The traditional back-front distinction as shown in figure 3.3 can be accounted for by a back-nonback distinction. Thus, *u, o, ɔ,* and *a* are classed as back, as against *i, æ,* and *e* which are nonback.

Round. As in traditional classifications, the rounding of the lips is a feature for vowel differentiation. Thus, for example, *u* is round, *i* nonround.

Note below how the vowel sounds of English are specified in terms of the foregoing features:

		Features			
Sound	*Example*	high	low	back	round
u	boot [but]	+	−	+	+
ɔ	bought [bɔt]	−	+	+	+
a	cot [kat]	−	+	+	−
o	boat [bo^{w}t]	−	−	+	+
i	beet [bi^{y}t]	+	−	−	−
æ	bat [bæt]	−	+	−	−
e	bait [be^{y}t]	−	−	−	−

Differentiation by Minimum Features

As we said earlier, the distinctive feature approach allows us to differentiate among speech sounds, and we have seen examples of this for the sounds of English. Figure 3.4 illustrates how this differentiation can be hierarchically arranged for these sounds. Notice how each sound is differentiated at the minimum from every other sound by at least one feature. The figure also illustrates how the features provide for the classification of sounds into categories— for example, obstruents, liquids, vowels, and so on.

Figure 3.5 illustrates how the phonetic realization of the sentence "The cats saw the mice" could be represented by a distinctive feature matrix. This representation also shows how continuous speech can be envisaged as a feature sequence. We will see later in this chapter how such a sequence has implications for physiological and psychological theories of speech production and perception.

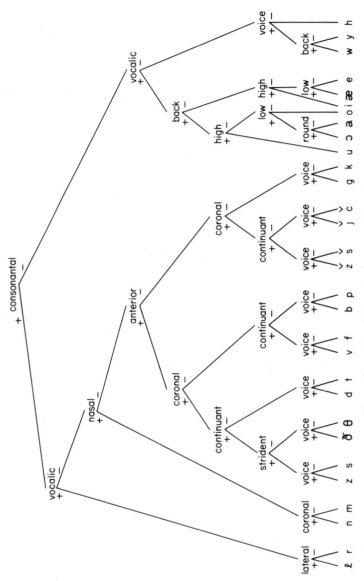

Figure 3.4 The distinctive features hierarchy.

	ð	e	#	k	æ	t	s	#	s	ɔ	#	ð	e	#	m	a	y	s
consonantal	+	−		+	−	+	+		+	−		+	−		+	−	−	+
vocalic	−	+		−	+	−	−		−	+		−	+		−	+	−	−
nasal	−	−		−	−	−	−		−	−		−	−		+	−	−	−
lateral																		
anterior	+			−		+	+		+			+			+			+
coronal	+			−		+	+		+			+			−			+
continuant	+			−		−	+		+			+			−			+
strident	−						+		+			−						+
voice	+			−		−	−		−			+					+	−
back		−			−				+			−				+	−	
high		−			−				−			−				−		
low		−			+				+			−				+		
round		−			−				+			−				−		
del. rel.	−	−		−	−	−	−		−	−		−	−		−	−	−	−

Figure 3.5   Distinctive features of sample utterance.

Production Dynamics

Most of what we have discussed thus far about speech production has involved the relatively static view of the articulatory configurations (gestures) for different speech sounds. Although this view tells us about the characteristics of speech sounds in more or less idealized descriptions, there remains a formidable challenge in describing the dynamics of articulation. One reason for this is that it is difficult to gather precise data about the activity of the articulating organs during normal speech. Given the evidence that we do have about articulatory dynamics, combined with implications drawn from the static descriptions of speech articulations and from our knowledge of the physiologic capabilities of the speech organs, it is possible to propose dynamic accounts of speech production. Although researchers and theorists do not agree on all the details of any such accounts, we can present a general outline of what is to be described.

Controls over Articulation

Linguistic instructions.   One question of any speech production theory is: What kinds of neuromuscular instructions control articulation? Here the emphasis is upon the nature of the instructions; we already know the nerves and muscles that are involved. As an approach to answers, we know for one thing that the instructions have to yield specific phonetic realizations. We already know some of the efficient ways to specify these outcomes, as in the use of distinctive features descriptions.

The problem with using relatively simple phonetic distinctions as articulatory instructions is that they cannot account for the variations in the dynamics of speech behavior, such as differences in transitions between sounds, and even differences in how sounds are made in variations in the speed of speech. These latter variations are significant enough to suggest that faster speech actually involves a somewhat different set of instructions to the articulators than slower speech. Accordingly, there must be some further type of instructions beyond purely linguistic ones which can account for such nonlinguistic factors as speech rate variations. Another example of nonlinguistic variations in production lies in how articulation varies relative to our breath supply. Again, there is the suggestion of controls that operate separate from, but in conjunction with, linguistically oriented instructions to the articulators.

Positional instructions. A more dynamically oriented account of articulatory controls incorporates the idea that instructions take into account the variations in positions that the articulators may be in prior to movement to a new or "target" sound. For example, the tongue movement needed for the production of *t* is partly dependent on whether the tongue was in a low back position for the production of the previous sound (e.g., *a*) or in a high front position (e.g., for *s*). In the former case, the instructions to the tongue muscles must involve moving the entire body of the tongue upward and forward. For *t* following *s*, no such instruction is necessary, but the muscles internal to the tongue must be instructed to flatten out the corona against the alveolar ridge.

The implication is that controls over articulation involve some combination of linguistically oriented rules which account for the targets of articulations as well as rules which take into account movements from prior targets to new ones. In a subsequent section of this chapter we will see further evidence of how instructions may relate the articulations of a prior sound to a later one, a phenomenon called *coarticulation*.

Feedback Capabilities

Another requirement of a production description lies in accounting for our capability to sense, if only subconsciously, the movements and positions of articulators during speech; that is, in accounting for *feedback* information.

Types of feedback. Four basic types of feedback are identified as *tactile, pressure, myotactic,* and *acoustic.* Tactile feedback is information concerning the contact between the articulating organs. Pressure feedback is information concerning the air pressure either in the oral cavity (as with obstruents) or in the subglottal chambers for all voiced sounds. Myotactic feedback is information concerning articulator positions, based upon our internal sensing of position and movement rather than tactile sensations—for example, as in our capability to touch our two index fingers with our eyes closed. Finally, acoustic feedback is our auditory perception of sounds as we make them, and as the sounds are transmitted either in the air or within the bony structures of our head.

Roles of feedback. Consonants, because they involve contact between the articulators and various types of air blockage, are the productions for which we can anticipate particular tactile and pressure feedback information. For example, we could consider the instruction and feedback information for *t* as: "Produce a gesture which creates a contact between the corona and the alveolar ridge and which causes air pressure to build up to a certain pressure behind the obstruction."

Vowels, by contrast, are more associated with myotactic feedback of tongue position and the acoustic information of the sound output resonance. Although acoustic information is relevant also to consonant production, their articulation appears to be too rapid for this information to be of as much feedback significance as tactile and pressure feedback. We can witness the general interference of acoustic feedback upon articulation when we have persons speak while equipped with a delayed-auditory-feedback device. As acoustic feedback is delayed for 0.20 sec or so, during speech, speakers typically begin to have trouble articulating correctly.

Physiologic Factors

Other aspects of the production process are suggested from studies directly examining the patterns of muscle behavior in the articulators. Such studies usually involve the use of X-ray movies of the speech organs, measures of the electrical activity within individual muscles, or both. Studies of electrical activity in muscles are known as *electromyographic* research.

Variations in muscle activity. Electromyographic studies have shown that the kind of muscular activity associated with vowels is quite different from that associated with consonants. For example, the lips are involved in the production of *p* and *b* as well as in the rounded vowels. The lip motion for the vowels is rather sluggish as compared to that of the consonants which is quick and abrupt.

In general it has been noticed that the consonants usually involve faster muscular gestures than do the vowels and, in many cases, entirely different sets of muscles are involved. Also, the smaller, more precise and faster-responding muscles are generally involved in the production of consonants. The larger, stronger muscles, such as those used to control the jaw and those external to the tongue but which control its position, are slower in response partly because they have heavier masses to move and partly because of the physiology of the muscle itself. It is believed that these are the muscles utilized chiefly in the production of vowels.

The distinction between the separate consonantal and vocalic muscular systems can be seen in the behavior of the tongue. The muscles internal to the tongue, some of which control the behavior of the corona of the tongue and form the groove necessary for the production of *s* and *z* sounds, are used primarily for the production of consonants. For the production of vowels, on the other hand, the muscles internal to the tongue are held in a relatively constant position, and the whole tongue is moved by the external large muscles to the proper position for the production of each vowel.

Coarticulation. In the study of speech production we can observe the anticipations of articulations, the phenomenon earlier labeled *coarticulation.* Compare your pronunciation of "two" and "tea." Note that when the closure is made for the *t* in "two," the lips are rounded in anticipation of the following vowel. When *t* is produced in the word "tea," however, the lips are spread in the anticipation of the *i*. This is an example of coarticulation.

For another example, compare your pronunciation of the following nonsense sequences: *ipi, apa,* and *upu.* During the production of the *p* in each of these sequences, the tongue is held in the position of the adjacent vowels. In fact, for *upu* the lips are even protruded during the production of the *p*. Moreover, they are spread in the case of the *p* in *ipi*. Here we can see the effect of coarticulation within the same organ, the lips. During the production of the bilabial closure, the configuration of the lips also reflects the characteristics of the adjacent vowels.

Some Final Notes

Further details of the dynamics of speech production would require far more space than is available here. Although we have relatively efficient ways to talk about the static representation of speech sounds in terms of their articulatory characteristics, a knowledge of their production dynamics, especially in the details of how the neural instructions operate, remains sketchy. These details are the topic of substantial contemporary research.

We have discussed mainly the production aspects of speech sounds, but nothing about how humans plan their overall utterances. After all, the sound sequence is but a phonetic representation of an utterance for which a speaker and listener typically share an associated meaning. Presumably, then, something to do with intended meaning, communication, or the like must precede the phonetic instructions for production, and we have not considered this here.

Perception Dynamics

Although perception and production of speech seem to call for a single type of explanation to account for the associations both speakers and listeners hold between sounds and meanings, their joint study usually stops at that point. The perception of speech sounds implies a *reception* capacity, that is, the transduction of the acoustic energy patterns of speech to the neural patterns transmitted by the stimulated auditory mechanism to the brain. We can talk about this transduction process in terms of theories of audition about which there is some, but not major, consensus. These theories focus upon recognition of acoustic qualities of pitch, loudness, and spectral pattern rather than upon the recognition of speech sounds. Accounts of the latter phenomenon are more linguistically oriented, and again, the concept of distinctive features aids us somewhat in describing some of the conditions of speech perception—at least of individual sounds and sound patterns. Beyond

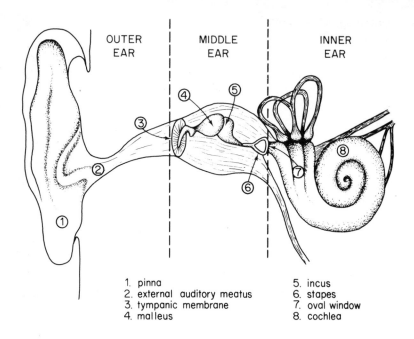

OUTER EAR	MIDDLE EAR	INNER EAR

1. pinna
2. external auditory meatus
3. tympanic membrane
4. malleus
5. incus
6. stapes
7. oval window
8. cochlea

cross sectional schematic of the cochlea

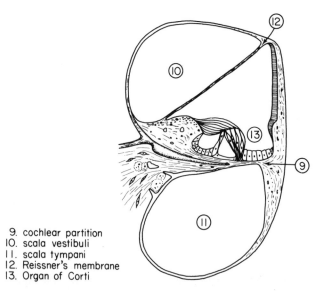

9. cochlear partition
10. scala vestibuli
11. scala tympani
12. Reissner's membrane
13. Organ of Corti

Figure 3.6   Simplified views of the auditory mechanism.

the perception of sounds, however, is the requirement for explaining how we interpret the meaning of an utterance. This problem, like the problem of explaining the planning of utterances, is left to the topic of psychological studies of language (Chapter 5).

Auditory Physiology

Figure 3.6 presents several simplified views of the auditory mechanism found in humans. As shown in the figure, the general divisions into the outer, middle, and inner ear are useful for descriptive purposes.

Outer ear. The external structure, or *pinna*, of the ear serves little function in the hearing capabilities of humans. The canal into the ear, or *external auditory meatus*, leads to the eardrum or *tympanic membrane*. Acoustic energy patterns in the air medium travel within the external auditory meatus, and due to the shape of this entryway there are resonance enhancements of frequencies ranging roughly from 3500 to 4000 cycles-per-second. Subsequently, the vibratory patterns of the acoustic energy are transduced to the (mechanical) vibration of the tympanic membrane.

Middle ear. The air-filled space of the middle ear contains three small bones (*ossicles*) which connect, and thus transmit vibratory movements between the tympanic membrane and another membrane called the *oval window*. These bones, called the *malleus*, *incus*, and *stapes*, are both connected and suspended by tiny ligaments. One apparent function of this ossicular chain is to magnify the pressure (force) component of the energy it transfers between the tympanic membrane and the oval window. Generally, it does this in two ways. First, because the force acting upon the tympanic membrane is concentrated from a larger area on this membrane to a smaller one on the oval window, the pressure component is enhanced. (This is akin to driving a nail into a board by the relative increase in driving pressure from the broader area of contact between the hammer and nail-head as compared with the area between the nail point and the board.) Second, the ossicular chain provides for a lever-action, somewhat akin to a crowbar-like action, that increases the force transmitted between the tympanic membrane and the oval window. Another function of the ossicular chain is that, to some degree, a dampening effect can protect the oval window from radical displacement due to very loud sounds.

Inner ear. The oval window marks the boundary to the inner ear, which is located within a small system of cavities of the skull. One bony labyrinth within this system where the vibrations of the oval window are converted to neural impulses is the *cochlea*. A spiral-shaped internal canal formed like a snail shell, the cochlea is divided into the *scala vestibuli* and *scala tympani*. The dividing structure is the *cochlear partition*. Figure 3.6 shows a cross section of the cochlear canal and its divisions. The cochlear partition itself has a duct which is separated from the scala vestibuli by *Reissner's membrane*. All of these canals are filled with fluid: *perilymph* in the scala vestibuli and scala tympani, and *endolymph* in the cochlear duct. Located on the *basilar membrane* in the cochlear partition is a markedly complex cluster of sensory cells known as the organ of *Corti*. As the oval window is displaced by movements of the stapes, this displacement is transmitted by movement of the fluid in the cochlea to the sensory (hair-like) cells of the organ of Corti. These sensations stimulate the fibers of the auditory nerve, and its signals are sent on to the brain.

Acoustic Perception

Although the physiology of the auditory mechanism is well known, the details of how the fluid movements in the cochlea and the corresponding neural excitations in the sensory cells of the organ of Corti allow us to differentiate among acoustic characteristics are not completely agreed upon by researchers. The general explanation accepted by most is called the *place-volley* theory which holds that we are able to sense acoustic characteristics in terms of a combination of two factors. One factor is the place in the array of sensory cells that is excited by a sound. The second factor is the frequency at which the cells are excited. This latter facet is what necessarily incorporates the volley portion of the theory because we are able to sense sounds that have a much higher acoustic frequency than the maximum neural firing rate. Just as a platoon of riflemen can exceed any one man's reloading rate if a few load while others fire, it is reasoned that sensory cells of hearing can be in different phases of firing and recovery so that the higher acoustic frequencies can be sensed.

Figure 3.7 summarizes the acoustic parameters of normal hearing. Although we can generally hear sounds from a frequency low of 20 cps to a high of 20,000 cps, note that for the lower sounds a relatively higher amplitude is required. Obviously, the sounds of speech would have to be within this "hearing" area, and indeed they are. The amplitude of normal conversation at about three feet between speakers is roughly 60 dB. Recall also that the frequency

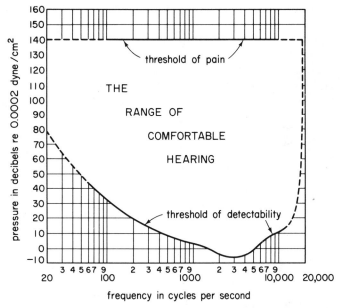

Figure 3.7 The hearing area.

band in the spectrograms of speech shown in Chapter 2 was between 200 and 7000 cps.

Speech Perception

Explanation of how we perceive the sounds of speech not only remains a challenge to researchers, but it also requires a very careful consideration of precisely what we are trying to take into account. As will be described, research has given some indications of what acoustic cues are important in the recognition of individual speech sounds. However, the same line of research has also raised serious doubts that our strategies for recognition of

individual sounds are significantly the same as when we are perceiving normal speech in a conversational situation. For present
purposes we will discuss several generalizations about the perception of individual sounds.

   Research by means of speech synthesis. Probably the most
productive research into the recognition of individual speech sounds
has been the "analysis-by-synthesis" approach. Here, the strategy
has been to take spectrographic patterns of speech sounds, to subject these patterns to experimental modifications, then to "play
"back the patterns as a kind of reconstituted (synthesized) speech.
An instrument called the *pattern playback* has been of key use in this
research. It works the opposite of a spectrograph; it takes spectrograms—usually hand-painted ones—as input, and furnishes their
acoustic realization as output. By a process of analyzing and
manipulating the spectral characteristics of speech sounds, then
synthesizing them back into acoustic form, researchers have found
some of the key cues to the perception of individual speech sounds.

   Figure 3.8 illustrates the type of results and implications of
analysis-by-synthesis research. By painting spectrograms which
could be replayed as sounds, researchers attempted to find the
minimum characteristics necessary for the recognition of the stop
consonants *b, d, g, p, t, k;* nasals *m, n, ŋ;* and the vowel *a.* The
patterns shown in figure 3.8 were the results. Note, for example,
how the differentiations of *b, d,* and *g* appear to depend upon the
initial characteristics of the second formant. (This is the only
characteristic which varies in the three spectral patterns.) Note
further that this generalization holds for the differentiation among the
unvoiced stops and among the nasals as well. That is, it is the initial
transition characteristics of the second formant which differentiates
among the voiced stops, the unvoiced stops, and the nasals. Figure
3.8 also illustrates how the results of speech recognition research
point back to the utility of classifying speech sounds in terms of their
manner and place of production.

   Some generalizations. The results of experiments such as
described above have led to a number of generalizations about the
recognition of types of speech sounds. We have already seen one of
these generalizations in how second formant transitions enable us
to differentiate among nasals and among voiced and unvoiced
stops. For vowels it has been found that the presence of two
formants is often enough for recognition, and the presence of three

guarantees it. It is the frequency relation among the formants that provides the key cues for vowel recognition and differentiation. The recognition of plosive consonants *p, t, k* depends upon the frequency of the initial burst relative to a following vowel sound. Fricative sounds such as *s* and *š* have greater intensities than the

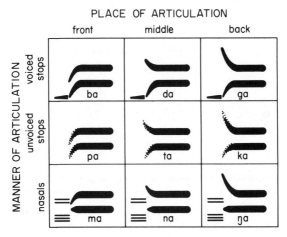

PLACE OF ARTICULATION

Fig. 2 Spectrographic patterns that illustrate the transition cues for the stop and nasal consonants in initial position with the vowel /a/. The dotted portions in the second row indicate the presence of noise (aspiration) in place of harmonics.

Figure 3.8   Some results of speech analysis by synthesis research (from Alvin M. Liberman, "Some Results of Research of Speech Perception," *Journal of the Acoustical Society of America*, 29, (1957): 117–23. Reprinted by permission).

fricatives *f* and θ, and the former are differentiated from each other in terms of the frequency concentration of their fricative-noise. Although there are more generalizations of this type which can be made, the point here is to illustrate the nature of such generalizations rather than summarizing all of them.

    Linguistic rules.   As in the discussion of speech production, it seems intuitively obvious that a listener's behavior with speech, like a speaker's, is somehow governed by his knowledge of the language. The crux of the matter is to find a way to describe the state or means

by which this knowledge exists in the mind of the speaker-listener
and how it is used in the perception (or production) process. It
would seem efficient or economical that the human speaker-listener
have a central type of linguistic knowledge that would apply to
both production and perception of speech. Unfortunately we lack
sufficient evidence at this time for testing the foregoing as a
hypothesis. At the least, we can say that such propositions are the
topic of contemporary research.

4 | Linguistic Perspectives

In Chapter 3 we concentrated on the sounds of language and man's capability for producing and receiving them. In this chapter we turn to that system which relates sounds to meanings—the system called *language*.

Speech is the performance of language, and language is the system of symbolism found in man's utterances. What is this system of symbolism? How can we identify it? How can we describe it? What is it that the speaker-listener uses when he uses language?

Some of the tentative answers to the above questions can be found in two contemporary approaches to the study of language. One of these approaches incorporates an observational and analytical strategy for discovering sound-meaning relations. Using this approach, called *descriptive linguistics*, we ask which distinctions in sounds and their patterns have correlations with meanings in a language. The second approach, more mentalistic and deductive in strategy, seeks to relate sounds and meanings through systems of rules. Using this approach, called *generative* (or *transformational*) *grammar*, we ask which rules can account for the generation of the grammatical (i.e., well-formed) sentences of a language.

We should note at the outset that descriptive and generative linguistics are not simply two alternative ways for studying language. As will be mentioned, generative grammar is intended as a new approach to linguistic theory and involves assumptions and aims quite different from descriptive linguistics. Although current advances in linguistic theory are mainly in generative grammar, an introduction to descriptive linguistics is necessary for an understanding of many traditional studies of speech behavior. Further, this introduction serves to emphasize the innovations of the generative approach. For this reason we will review both the more traditional and new approaches to linguistic study in this chapter.

The Descriptive Approach

Much of what is discussed in this section represents an approach typically called descriptive or structural linguistics. As this label implies, the goal in descriptive linguistics is to provide a systematic identification, classification, and labeling of linguistic phenomena.

Introductory Concepts

Expression and content systems. The descriptive linguist makes a fundamental distinction between what is called the *expression system*, the specific kinds of sounds and their sequences in a language, and the *content system* (the kinds of distinctions in what these sounds and their sequences mean, or signify, to their users). Most of descriptive linguistics is devoted to the analysis of the expression system, while the content system is used as an aid to fulfill this intent. Although the descriptive linguist may often talk about meaning (as in discussing vocabularies, word referents, or his bases for speech analyses), he does not typically undertake a description of the content system itself. In short, he avoids the problem of describing the meaning system. Analogous to this approach is the task of the communications engineer who is concerned with the electronic code that, for example, unites two teletype machines. He will have to know something about, but not necessarily describe, the contents of the messages sent by this system in order to describe fully (or "break") the code. When the linguist asks a person (*informant*) whether the expressive difference between "bat" and "pat" signifies difference to him in meaning, he is using content to determine symbolically significant distinction in expression.

The structural hierarchy of expression systems. It is essential to consider how the expression system of language has both a sequential and a hierarchical organization. Note in figure 4.1 how the utterance "The cats saw the mice" can be divided into different types of units or structures. We can consider, for example, how this sentence represents a sound sequence in the acoustic spectrum. Or we can represent the sounds in terms of the phonetic transcription used in Chapter 3. Above the phonetic transcription we

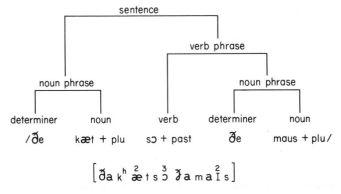

Figure 4.1 Levels of linguistic analysis.

have written in the basic types of English sounds that represent the linguistic identification of these sounds in the *phonemes* of English. When we are studying the sounds of utterances from a linguistic standpoint, we are dealing with what is called *phonology*.

Notice, however, how certain sounds and clusters of sounds enter into the words of the sentence. As we will discuss later, descriptive linguists are not typically interested in words themselves but in word-like basic sounds (e.g., "s") or clusters of sounds ("cat + s") which have particular correlations with meanings in the content system. These basic expressive units are called *morphemes*, and their study *morphology*. Finally, we can consider in this example how the morphemes in turn fit into further types of constructions called *phrases*, and how combinations of phrases make up sentences. The study of such constructions is called *syntax*. In sum, it is important to recognize how the phonologic, morphologic, and syntactic aspects of the expression system are used by the descriptive linguist to characterize the hierarchical organization of language. In descriptive linguistics, we are typically interested in these three levels, which we will next review in more detail.

Phonology

   Phonemics. In Chapter 3 we saw that phonemics involved the identification of the basic sound segments (i.e., phonemes) of a language, and that distinctive features could be used as a classification scheme. To continue the discussion of phonemes at this point, one way to illustrate what is meant by "basic sound segments" is to consider the contrasts shown in *minimal pairs.*

   Suppose, for illustration, that you are asked whether "bat" and "pat" mean different things to you. If you answer yes, then this is evidence that "b" and "p" may be functioning as phonemes in your phonologic system. We can tell by our auditory observation that there is a sound difference between "bat" and "pat" and that this difference is essentially in the "b–p" distinction. This is called finding a *minimal pair.* If "b" and "p" are phonemes in your expression system, then (1) we would expect to find further words in your expression system that are distinguished from one another in terms of only the "b–p" expressive distinction, and (2) we will find no expression examples in your language where the "b–p" distinction is broken into some still more detailed distinction in a minimal pair.

   For the first criterion, then, we would expect to find expressive distinctions such as "bin–pin," "bill–pill," and "pit–bit," all of which should have distinctions in your content system. To illustrate the second criterion, suppose that we had initially observed a distinction between "bat" and "spat." We might at first think that the "b" and "sp" is a minimal pair. This might be suggested, at first, by such example as "bar–spar," or by "bit–spit." But because such distinctions as "bar–par" or "bit–sit" exist, we know that in your expression system the "b–sp" distinction is not a basic one because there exist "b–p" and "b–s" distinctions, and even "s–p" ("sit–pit") distinctions. That is, more minimal distinctions are to be found than the "b–sp" distinction.

   Allophones. We have already said that phonemes are categories of sounds and that this implies that there may be some sound variations among expressions of a given phoneme. When differing sounds are assigned to the same phoneme in a language they are called *allophones.* The determination of allophones is an important facet of phonemic analysis because it sometimes serves in the determination of what is a phonemic distinction. Consider, for example, the difference between the words "scat" and "cat" or "skate" and "kate" in English. In the first word of each of these pairs the sound [k] is articulated without a burst of air as a part of the sound, whereas in the second of each of these pairs the sound has this aspirated quality [k^h]. These two sounds are allophones of the /k/ phoneme in English.[1] A useful point about this distinction is that in English the [k] and [k^h] sounds never occur in the same phonetic context. (Try to say "scat" with a burst of air after the [k] as in "cat.") If these two versions of this sound can never appear in the same type of phonologic context, then it follows that they could never form a phonemic distinction in English. If they were, we might find words that differed from one another in no other way than the [k]–[k^h] distinction, and this is impossible because these two sounds never occur in the same linguistic context in English. In short, if we can demonstrate an allophone, we have at the same time demonstrated that we do not have a phonemic distinction.

    Segmentals and suprasegmentals. The types of phonemes that we have discussed thus far are typically called *segmentals*, because essentially we have located them by dividing the speech sequence into segments. A summary listing of the segmental phonemes of English was given in table 3.1. We can add to these segmentals further types of sound distinctions which have correlates in distinctions of meaning but are expressive distinctions which occur simultaneously with segmental phonemes or sometimes along with them as stress or intonation phenomena. These are called *suprasegmentals*. Suprasegmentals of English are summarized below:

> Stress: primary /′/, secondary /ˆ/, tertiary /ˋ , weak /ˇ/
> Open transition or break: /+/
> Pitch: low /1/, mid /2/, high /3/, extra-high /4/
> Clause terminals: fading / /, rising /↗/, sustained /→/

Some example transcriptions using suprasegmentals are:

$$\overset{\;\;2}{\text{What are you doing}} + \overset{3}{\text{Dad}}↗$$

$$\overset{3}{\text{I'm in the greenhouse planting turnips}}↘$$

---

[1] Again, where the distinction is important for clarity, phonetic symbols appear in brackets, phonemes between slashes.

Distinctive features. As already discussed in Chapter 3, phonemes can be defined in terms of bundles of phonetic features and contrasted with one another according to distinctive features. Descriptive linguistics has typically incorporated the phoneme as the basic element of the phonological system of language, although the description of phonemes in terms of phonetic or distinctive features is not at odds with this idea. However, current advances in phonological theory within generative grammar focus almost exclusively upon the concept of distinctive features. In fact, it is questioned whether the phoneme is a useful linguistic concept.

Morphology

Phonemes compared with morphemes. In phonology we saw how distinctions in the minimal sound units of the expression system provided a basis for distinctions in the content system. In morphology we are concerned with finding minimum *particular utterances* in the expression system that have a relation with *particular meanings* in the content system of a language. We can see the distinction between phonology and morphology by referring to the Morse Code. What we observe as dots and dashes in the code are phonemes as in a phonologic system, but what those dots and dashes and their patterns mean is an example of identifications on the morphologic level. To turn to a language example, the sound [e] in English is phonemic, but when it occurs as the article "a" as in "a house," it goes beyond having just a sound distinction in English to having a correlation with a particular meaning in this language. In short, it signifies a morpheme. On the other hand, when [e] occurs within a word such as "bait," it is only serving as one of a number of phonemes which together constitute a morpheme.

The objective in morphemic description is the identification of the smallest units in the expression system that can be correlated with specific meanings in the content system. Calling morphemes the smallest unit implies that a given morpheme cannot be divided into still smaller units and retain its correlation with content. Bear in mind, however, that the objective in morphology is still to describe the expression system, not the content system.

Free and bound forms. The method for identifying the morphemes of a language mainly involves finding contrasts between pairs of utterances that include differences in expression (actual sound differences or differences in where they can occur in the linguistic context) which correlate with differences in content Consider these examples:

(i) "cat"
(ii) "cats"

Example (i) cannot be divided into any smaller units that maintain some consistent relation with meaning in the English language content system. This kind of a morpheme is called a *minimal form*. It is also known as a *free form* morpheme because it can occur in the absence of any other form. That is, it can stand alone. It is also called a *stem* because other morphemes can be added to it to somehow modify its basic meaning, as is the case in example (ii). Here the morpheme -*s*, indicating plural in English, has been added to the stem. Morphemes which only appear as additions to other morphemes are called *bound forms* (as contrasted with *free* forms) or *affixes*. Bound forms occur as *suffixes* when they follow the stem (as in the example just given), as *prefixes* when they precede the stem (as in "renew"), and in languages other than English as *infixes* when they occur within the stem morpheme.

Distribution. Morphemes can be classified according to the kinds of linguistic context in which they can occur. One example of this is that bound forms only occur when affixed with other morphemes. Another example is illustrated in the contrast between morphemes "cat" and "saw." We could say "The cats saw the mice," or "The mice saw the cat," but not "The saw cats the mice." As shown in this example, and as you already know, nouns and verbs occur in different linguistic contexts. In short, all morphemes can be classed in terms of their distributional characteristics.

Homophony. Some different morphemes have the same sound; that is, they are *homophonous*. Consider, for example, *s* in the words "cats" and "thinks." The *s* on the first word indicates a plural morpheme that may be assigned to English nouns, whereas the *s* on the second word indicates a verb in the third person singular form. Although the *s* sound is the same in both cases, its morphemic role depends upon the linguistic context. This example illustrates homophonous morphemes, as well as another type of contextual classification.

Allomorphs. It is also possible for a single morpheme to have different ways to be expressed phonologically; these different expressions are called *allomorphs.* Some allomorphic variation is considered to be *free.* There are no definable linguistic conditions for predicting or describing the variation. For example, the suffix [-ing] shows free variation between "-in" [-in] and "-ing" [-iŋ] in the speech of many, as in "workin" or "thinkin." Such allomorphs have free variation, but as we will see in Chapter 6, there may be ways of predicting such a variation depending upon the speech situation, the speaker, or the formality of his speech.

Another type of allomorphic variation is called *phonologic conditioning.* This is when the particular expressive form of a morpheme is predictable upon the basis of the phonological context within which it occurs. Compare how the expression of the English noun plural morpheme varies in "cats," [-s], "foxes" [ɨz], and "tags" [-z]. These varied expressions are allomorphs of the same morpheme, and we can describe their variation according to the stem ending. For example, /-s/ occurs after voiceless sounds such as in "cups," "cuts," or "packs"; whereas /-ɨz/ occurs after stem endings as in "classes," "fezzes" or "edges"; and /-z/ occurs after voiced sounds as in "cubs," "fads," "bags," and so on.

Another type of allomorph is one which is said to be *morphologically conditioned.* This is where the particular means for expressing a bound form morpheme may vary with the specific type of morpheme with which it is combined, as when we say "oxen," "geese," or "mice."

For notational purposes, we can represent all of the above variations in noun plural allomorphs by use of a single symbol. In English the noun plural morpheme, no matter what its means of expression, is typically identified as $\{Z_1\}$. The subscript distinguishes this class of morpheme from other noun affixes, such as where $\{Z_2\}$ indicates a suffix for possessives in English (e.g., "dog's").

Obviously, much of what is said here about morphology is a way to discuss linguistically the make-up of what we refer to as "words." In descriptive linguistics the morpheme provides a more exacting concept of a relation between expression and meaning which can be related to phonemes, on the one hand, and to the pattern sequences of language on the other. Morphemes lead systematically into the next level of description, that is, to syntax.

Syntax

Structural parts. Usually our concern with syntax ranges from those types of structures that have morphemes as constituent units, then to structural units which combine, layer upon layer, until we reach a maximum type of construction, typically called the *sentence.* This is a part of language description that most readers are apt to remember from their primary and secondary school days. The sentence, "The cats saw the mice" in some school grammars would have been described in terms of the sequence:

determiner + noun + verb + determiner + noun

or

subject phrase + verb + direct object

Identifications such as these attempt to account for the kinds of units which go into the different constructional patterns of English, or for that matter the constructional patterns of any language. In syntax the hierarchical aspect of language organization is particularly important to us. One of the usual ways to define this hierarchical organization, as well as a way of discovering it in sentences, is discussed next.

Immediate constituent analysis. In immediate constituent analysis we are concerned with how syntactic units, called constructions, are made up of pairs of subordinate syntactic units, or constituents. We could say, for example, that the sentence construction, "The cats saw the mice," could be divided into two main immediate constituents (as in Fig. 4.1). The subject noun phrase, "the cats" is one constituent unit and the verb phrase "saw the mice" is another. We would say that these two phrase units of the sentence are the immediate constituents of the overall sentence (a construction). In turn we can divide these phrases into their own immediate constituents. Thus "the" and "cats" are the immediate constituents of the subject noun phrase construction described above, and "saw" plus the direct object phrase "the mice" are the immediate constituents of the verb phrase construction. Finally, the object phrase can be divided into its own immediate constituents "the" and "mice." We have thus divided the sentence as a construction into successive levels of immediate constituents. We could describe these successive levels of immediate constituents in terms of what is called a "tree diagram" (Fig. 4.1).[2]

The basic guide for immediate constituent analysis is to know where to divide the construction in each of the steps of subdivision. Although linguists differ on criteria for subdivision, we can illustrate some of the criteria that are commonly used. One of the first is that constructions can typically be divided into *two* immediate constituents. Binary division is followed unless there is some strong reason to suggest an alternative, such as dividing the direct objects in the sentence "The boy hit Fred, Jim, and Bill." Other criteria reflect the modification patterns thought to be identified in the sentence. For example, consider where the first division would be in the phrase "the big boy." One could argue that since "big" goes together in a modification pattern with "boy," and that "the" modifies the combination of "big boy," then the first division should be between "the" and the two-word phrase which it modifies. This assumes, of course, that we know beforehand some of the typical modification patterns of the language, and that we can bring these modification patterns to bear in making decisions about immediate constituent division.

Also reflected in the above illustration is the criterion called *substitutability*. Here we ask which subdivision of a construction would result in the selection of immediate constituents, either of which could be replaced maximally independent of one another. That is, which division will result in parts where these parts could have the maximum number of possible replacements. As in the example above, we would make the first division between "the" and the phrase "big boy," and the second division between "big" and "boy." Presumably, "the" could have a maximum substitutability with the phrase "big boy," and this phrase, likewise, would have maximum substitutability relative to its immediate constituent "the." At least these parts would allow more substitutions than an initial division of "the big" and "boy." A good review of the different criteria for making immediate constituent divisions is presented by Street (1967).

---

[2] We could go further to divide cats and mice into their stem + plural forms. A tree diagram of this appears in figure 4.3.

Research Method

Descriptive linguistics is strictly empirical in method. Statements are made only about what can be directly observed, and what can be tested again and again by returning to the language data or behaviors which are under observation. In studying an undescribed language, the descriptive linguist typically works with an informant who is considered to be a fluent speaker of that language. The linguist can then take sample utterances of the language and by asking the informant whether they mean the same or different things, he can eventually develop phonologic, morphologic, and syntactic descriptions of that language. Introductory texts in descriptive linguistics are those by Hockett (1958) and Gleason (1961); a text on American English is provided by Gleason (1965).

The Generative View

Another way of describing language, and an even different way for conceptualizing the description itself, is the generative view, an approach most associated with the transformational grammar of Chomsky (1957, 1965). We will discuss a few of the fundamental concepts which make this view a radical departure from descriptive linguistics. Subsequently we will use simplified examples to illustrate how syntactic and phonologic aspects of language can be described in terms of the generative view.

Some Fundamentals

Goals of a generative grammar. The objective in generative grammar is more one of development of linguistic theory than a method for describing particular languages. This objective was expressed in Chomsky's small volume, *Syntactic Structures* (1957) which set forth the goals and a tentative outline for a new linguistic theory. Chomsky was dissatisfied with descriptive linguistics, since, in his thinking, its development pointed more toward a system for the classification of linguistic phenomena, rather than an approach which would eventually lead to a theory of language. Chomsky was not only dissatisfied with the contemporary methods of linguistics, but argued that we could never have an adequate theory of language if it had to be based upon a strictly empirical approach. By contrast, he argued that a linguistic theory should describe the kind of knowledge that would be necessary in order to create and understand the sentences of a language. Presumably some of this knowledge was of a universal order (it applied to all languages) whereas other portions of this knowledge would be specific to a given language.

Linguistic competence as compared with performance. As a theoretical model, Chomsky conceives of the *ideal* speaker-listener. This is a conception of a language user where the sole consideration is the nature of linguistic knowledge. There is no concern with the factors of performance such as memory capacity, the details of speech circumstances, or the motives for creating or reacting to utterances. Having avoided these behavioral concerns, the objective is then to describe the type of knowledge this ideal speaker-listener would have to have in order to create and understand the sentences of a language. Chomsky calls this knowledge *linguistic competence.* In generative linguistic theory, linguistic competence is described in terms of a system of syntactic, semantic, and phonologic rules. The collection of such rules in Chomsky's definition is called the *grammar* of a language.

The rules of a generative grammar, by assumption, cannot be directly observed in speakers. On the contrary, the generative grammarian develops rules (1) from what the universal aspects of the grammar (i.e., aspects applicable to all languages) would imply for a specific language, (2) from what the linguist's knowledge of his language indicates to him about the grammaticality of sentences, and (3) from the linguist's observation of whether the proposed rules lead to the expected types of sentences in the production and comprehension behaviors of language users. Just as the mathematician can deduce and symbolically manipulate the rules of addition without observing how people behave when they add, the generative grammarian tries to deduce the rules of a language without necessarily observing all of the details of performance. In fact, relative to a generative grammar, description of language behavior is left to a separate theory of *performance.* In Chomsky's terms, describing competence is the task of the linguist, whereas describing performance is the task of the psycholinguist. We will see more about the nature of performance in Chapter 5.

Components of the grammar. A complete generative grammar of a language would relate the sounds of that language to its meanings through components comprising phonologic, syntactic, and semantic rules. Most of Chomsky's writings (1957, 1965) have dealt with the syntactic component of grammar, although more recently the phonology of English and other languages has been studied (Chomsky and Halle, 1968) in some detail. Only highly speculative versions of the semantic component of a generative grammar exist (Katz and Fodor, 1963).

For purposes of illustration, we will develop some very simplified examples of syntactic and phonologic rules of English.

Syntactic Component

At the heart of a generative grammar are those rules that generate the constructional hierarchy of a sentence. We will illustrate how rules can be used to account for this hierarchy.

Rule forms. Assume that the grammar will be made upon rules that have the following form:

$$X \rightarrow Y$$

This generalized form means that whatever element is identified as an "X" (i.e., will fit an "X" in the rule) is to be rewritten as "Y." Or put another way, we could say that for a given "Y," the rewrite rule would tell us about the underlying "X". For now we will place some restrictions upon what can be substituted for "X" and "Y". Also, we will keep track of these restrictions by saying that only elements identified by capital letters can be "X", whereas elements identified by either capital or lower case letters can be "Y". One implication of this restriction at this point is that whenever the rule yields an element having a lower case letter we can no longer rewrite that same element (because the lower case letter cannot be an "X"). Accordingly, we will call the lower case symbols *terminal elements.*

In order for the grammar to have a starting point, we will give it an *initial element,* labeled *S,* which indicates the format for a sentence in our simple grammar.

Phrase structure rules (PS).   Rules of the PS type will define the major structure of sentences; a set of such rules, or the *grammar* itself, is given in figure 4.2.   Note that PS rules have the form that X is always identified with a single symbol (capital letters), and that the rewrite (Y) represents an expansion of some type. Note also

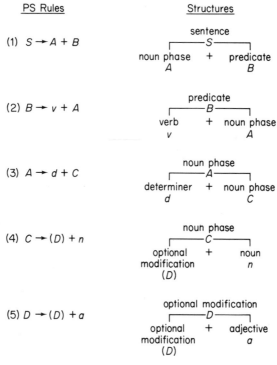

<u>PS Rules</u>   <u>Structures</u>

(1) $S \rightarrow A + B$

sentence
$\lceil$————S————$\rceil$
noun phase   +   predicate
     A   B

(2) $B \rightarrow v + A$

predicate
$\lceil$————B————$\rceil$
verb   +   noun phase
  v   A

(3) $A \rightarrow d + C$

noun phase
$\lceil$————A————$\rceil$
determiner + noun phase
    d   C

(4) $C \rightarrow (D) + n$

noun phase
$\lceil$————C————$\rceil$
optional   +   noun
modification   n
  (D)

(5) $D \rightarrow (D) + a$

optional modification
$\lceil$————D————$\rceil$
optional   +   adjective
modification   a
  (D)

Figure 4.2   A simplified grammar.

that we have identified the terminal elements in the sample grammar as syntactic units akin to parts of speech in the surface sequence of a sentence. (Although generative grammars do not involve parts of speech as such, they do incorporate designations of a surface syntactic sequence.)

Each PS rule in the grammar corresponds to one of the syntactic layers described earlier for a sentence of the type, "The cats saw the mice." PS-rule 1 $(S \rightarrow A + B)$ represents the rewrite of the initial symbol into immediate constituents: noun phrase and verb phrase. PS-rule 2 $(B \rightarrow v + A)$ rewrites the predicate verb phrase into the verb and noun phrase. PS-rule 3 $(A \rightarrow d + C)$ accounts for one layer of the construction of noun phrases. But note that PS-rule 3 results in one terminal symbol (d), which means that we will not have to rewrite (for now) this element further. PS-rule 4 $(C \rightarrow (D) + n)$ defines another layer of the noun phrase, and PS-rule 5 $(D \rightarrow (D) + a)$ the last layer. Rule 4 has given us another terminal symbol (n), which leaves the (D) element yet to be rewritten. Rule 5 handles this final rewriting, but along with rule 4 also gives us an option (shown by the parenthesis around D) of using D again and recycling back to rule 5. As we shall see, this option will provide for the addition of multiple adjectives prior to the nouns in the sentence, or for the use of no adjectives at all. Now let us see how the five rules could result in, or account for the underlying structure of, sentences having the form of the sample sentence.

Any sentence having a part of speech sequence which could follow from (be generated) by the rules in figure 4.2 would, by the terms of the sample grammar, be *grammatical*. By the same token, any sentence having a syntactic sequence not accountable by the grammar would be *ungrammatical*. Thus "The saw cat the mice" is ungrammatical because the grammar does not provide for that syntactic sequence. But we would consider a sentence such as "The jar ate the wall" as grammatical because it follows from the syntactic rules, even though it is a semantic anomaly.

PS-rule 5 illustrates one of the advantages of the generative method of syntactic description in how it accounts for the syntactic quality known as *recursiveness*. This refers to the options that the grammar gives us for adding additional adjectives in the modification of nouns. Figure 4.2 illustrates how this recursiveness operates with PS-rule 5. As illustrated, the addition of adjectives involves simply the taking of the option provided by (D) in rule 4 and re-applying rule 5 so long as there are adjectives to be added. Thus with this type of rule, a sentence such as "The great big old man hit the old musty worn ball" is grammatical. In fact, under the rules of this simplified grammar, as in some of the PS-rules of English, it is theoretically possible (but limited practically in performance) to have an infinite number of adjectives modifying a noun.

Transformational rules (T). Whereas the PS-rule in our simplified grammar only take single elements (X) as input, T-rules take entire sequences or symbol strings as X and rewrite them into some rearrangement with possible additions or deletions. We will add one T-rule to our grammar; it is:

$$(\text{T-rule 6}) \quad A + v + A' \rightarrow A' + \text{was} + v + \text{by} + A$$

As illustrated in figure 4.3, T-rule 6 gives us the capability of transforming the surface sequence of our simple sentence from an active

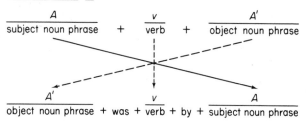

Structural change:

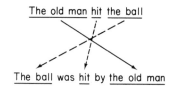

Example:

Figure 4.3   A transformational rule.

form into a passive one. Thus our simple grammar can account for the underlying syntactic structure of such sentences as, "The white baseball was hit by the baseball player" or "The old, old, old man was saved by the young, heroic boy."

In a general sense, PS-rules are typically said to account for the major underlying, or *deep*, structure of sentences, whereas transformational rules account for variations in surface structure. Although there are many more details than we have illustrated here, the distinction between PS and T-rules is generally accurate. The nature of PS and T-rules illustrates why this linguistic viewpoint is typically called a generative or generative-transformational grammar.

Phonological Component

In Chapter 3 we saw how the phonemes of a language could be differentiated from one another in terms of the *distinctive feature* approach. In a generative grammar the phonological unit contains rules which take the surface structure result of the syntactic component, then further rewrite it in terms of a series of distinctive features, yielding the phonetic composition of the sentence. An illustration of phonological rules is provided by a consideration of the phonologically conditioned allomorphs of the English noun plural morpheme. If we consider, for example, the different phonologic versions of this morpheme, it should be evident that we could use rules such as the following to describe the variations of -*s* endings:

(1) Plu → /ɨz/ in environment: {s, z, š, ž, č, ǰ} + ——
(2) Plu → /s/ in environment: {p, t, k, θ, f} + ——

$$(3) \quad \text{Plu} \rightarrow /z/ \text{ in environment:} \begin{Bmatrix} \text{l, r, n, m, d, ð,} \\ \text{v, b, g, u, ɔ, a,} \\ \text{o, i, æ, ŋ, e, w, y} \end{Bmatrix} + \text{——}$$

These rules account for essentially the same sorts of descriptive statements as were summarized earlier in the discussion about noun plural -*s* allomorphs (but not irregulars such as geese, mice, oxen, etc.). Rule 1 specifies that the plural is /ɨz/ whenever the noun stems to which it is attached ends in one of /s, z, š, ž, č, ǰ/. Similarly, rules 2 and 3 specify the variations according to given stem contexts. The braces around the set of environmental (stem) phonemes indicates an optional choice of any member inside the braces. The plus sign (+) indicates a morpheme boundary. The dash (——), called the *environment bar*, specifies the context in which the plural morpheme must be found in order for the rule to apply.

The applications of these rules are illustrated in the derivations shown below:

Stems:	buš + Plu	kæp + Plu	rib + Plu
Rule-1	buš + ɨz	——	——
Rule-2	——	kæp + s	——
Rule-3	——	——	rib + z

Here we see that the noun stem *bush* provides an environment which triggers the application of rule 1. When the plural morpheme follows a /p/, as in the word *cap*, rule 2 applies. Rule 3 is applicable for the word *rib*.

These rules (1, 2, 3) are obviously cumbersome. We can improve upon their representation by using distinctive features. For example, the phonemes (s, z, š, ž, č, ǰ) in the environment for rule 1 are all and only those which are both *strident* and *coronal* (Chapter 3). A next consideration is that the phonemes in the environment for rule 2 are the remaining voiceless phonemes. It might appear at first incorrect to refer to the class of phonemes in rule 2 by only the feature *unvoiced*, because such a specification would also include /s, š, č/ of rule 1. If, however, we assume that rule 1 will apply *prior to* the application of rule 2, then when rule 2 applies, all of these plural morphemes which had originally been in the environment appropriate for rule 1 will have already been converted from the "Plu" representation in the phoneme sequence and would not apply to rule 2. Thus there would be no possibility for rule 2 applying to a plural morpheme affixed to a noun stem which ends in one of /s, š, č/. We see, then, that ordering the rules makes it possible to refer to the class of phonemes which makes up the environment for rule 2 merely by the feature *unvoiced*.

The order of these rules also offers a great economy in the representation of rule 3. Here it is no longer necessary to specify *any* environment whatsoever. This is because rule 3 simply applies in all those environments which had not been already specified for rules 1 and 2. In all, using distinctive features in the environment and ordering our rules enables us to restate the three rules in the following greatly simplified form:

(1) Plu → /ɨz/ in environment: $\begin{Bmatrix} \text{strident} \\ \text{coronal} \end{Bmatrix}$ + ——

(2) Plu → /s/ in environment: {unvoiced} + ——

(3) Plu → /z/ in any environment.

The examples above illustrate two main ways that using distinctive features in phonological rules provides an economical description. First, by using distinctive features, it is possible to refer to large classes of phonemes by means of a very few features. Second, great economy can be achieved by ordering rules. The generative phonologist seeks the most general and economical set of rules to comprise the phonological component of a grammar. This is an ordered set of phonological rules which can refer by distinctive features to such grammatical markers as noun pluralization, lexical items, transformation of lexical items, and sentence intonation. The output of such rules can be conceived in terms of the distinctive feature sequence of speech.

5 | Psychological Perspectives

It is one thing to talk about the complexities of language, yet it seems an even greater challenge to describe how the human being is capable of using these complexities. Some type of neural signals must control the articulators, and presumably some type of language planning must precede this control. Similarly, auditory stimulation is only a first step in what must be a complex series of neural events that comprise the perception of an utterance and the behaviors which are functions of such perception. In the broadest view, the question posed about the psychology of the language user is how man creates and understands utterances. We shall see, however, that in terms of specific psychological theories of the language user, answers to this question and even the question itself, become altered, depending upon points of view the different theorists take concerning what is important in the description of language behavior.

A Continuum of Viewpoints

Figure 5.1 illustrates several of the major contrasts among different psychological theories of the language user. On the one hand, there are theories where generalizations are based only upon those facets of language behavior that can be directly observed. These theories avoid speculation about internal (especially cognitive) processes involved in language behavior. They typically focus upon situations where the observable stimulus, response, or both, involve language behavior. Such theories are aptly called *behavioristic*, since they reflect this rigorously observational school of psychology.

By contrast there are theories of the language user, such as is shown in the center of figure 5.1, where speculations are made about internal (*mediational*) processes in language behavior. In theories of this type, researchers are concerned not only with the definition of stimulus and response events but also the types of

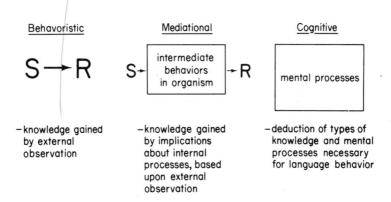

Figure 5.1   Theories of the language user.

internal behaviors that link the series of events that take place in the organism from its stimulation to its response. These theories are typically called *mediational* because most of their generalizations are about behaviors that are intermediate between stimulation and response of the organism.

Finally, there is an approach where the concern is mainly in trying to develop an explanation of the mental process that would have to take place in order to create and interpret linguistic utterances. This approach, called the *cognitive*, places least stress upon observation, and most stress upon the explanatory power of generalizations made about language performance.

As you might well imagine, researchers differ in their criteria for evaluating theoretical statements made in the behavioristic, mediational, or cognitive theories of the language user. Obviously, too, there are quite different bases for developing generalizations for these different theoretical approaches. In short, expect to find marked differences among the theories to be discussed.

Skinner's Behavioristic Theory

Background

In the opening pages of *Verbal Behavior* (1957), B. F. Skinner argues that most of the shortcomings of prior attempts to create adequate theories of verbal behavior have been due to the insurmountable problems encountered in trying to study the internal process loosely referred to as *meaning*. As a behaviorist, Skinner considers that meaning does not lend itself to systematic observation since it is a covert (internal) type of behavior. As a behaviorist, Skinner was also concerned with developing a causal picture relative to verbal behavior—that is, how might verbal behavior be best described within a stimulus-response framework? Accordingly, Skinner set out to develop a theoretical framework for verbal behavior that would both avoid the problem of meaning and would enlarge upon this causal picture.

The Verbal Situation

Response conditioning. At the center of Skinner's theorizing is the kind of behavioral situation in which language is typically involved. The basic framework for describing this situation is one of a conditioning or learning paradigm—that is, a situation in which stimulus and response become linked. Figure 5.2 outlines the major constituents of the verbal situation. To see the dynamics of this situation, suppose that a human being in a given motivational

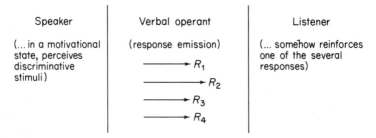

Figure 5.2   Operant conditioning paradigm.

state has emitted a variety of overt (external) behaviors, as indicated by R_{1-4} in figure 5.2. Suppose further that another human somehow responded to one of these overt behaviors and satisfied the speaker's motivational state. Under the assumptions of learning theory, such need-satisfaction, reward, or reinforcement, would increase the probability that one of the different behaviors would occur again in that same need situation. Thus, eventually when the initiating organism (or the speaker) is in a given need state, he will likely emit a certain response (e.g., R_2) and that response will lead to an anticipated reinforcement. In sum, a particular kind of verbal response which is reinforced (conditioned) under a particular situation will eventually lead to the emission of that same response in future cases where the same need or stimulus situation exists.

Verbal operants. The foregoing types of responses which are predictable within given need situations are called *operants* in Skinner's theory. What makes an operant a *verbal* operant, according to Skinner, is that its reinforcement depends upon the behavior of a listener (or audience). As an example of such situations, we could consider that a speaker's need state might range all the way from such physical needs as thirst or hunger to a more generalized type of social need of simply gaining approval or avoiding disapproval. The *discriminative stimuli* (or *stimulus*) in the situation are the phenomena relevant to this motivational state. For example, if the speaker is thirsty, relevant stimuli would be the presence of water and someone to provide the speaker with a glass of it. The verbal operant is then the speaker's request for water. Its reinforcement is when he actually receives this water. A more subtle situation could involve a mother speaking a word to her child. Both the mother and her utterance are discriminative stimuli. The need state is the child's motivation to gain approval from the mother. The operant could be the child's repetition of a word. Reinforcement is then provided by the mother's overt approval of this— for example, a smile or a pat.

In a general sense, then, language behavior is viewed by Skinner as conditioned responses to different types of verbal situations. In the course of language development the language user gains a repertoire of these types of responses as a function of their reinforcement in given need situations. Speech development is an expanding repertoire of verbal operants. As Skinner elaborates this basic paradigm, he is mainly concerned with a description of the different types of verbal operants and eventually how these combine as complex behaviors in situations of actual language usage.

Types of Verbal Operants

Essentially, different verbal operants are defined in terms of the kinds of situations in which they occur, and in particular, how the specific operant serves a functional role within that situation. Because this functional role is a key to Skinner's theorizing, the assessment of verbal behavior along these lines is sometimes called a *functional analysis*. The different operants in Skinner's theory are defined in terms of their functional roles within the verbal situations. He has coined terms to name some of these operants.

Mands and tacts. Verbal operants called *mands* function directly as a consequence of the need state of the organism. In fact, one can observe that the mand operant specifies its reinforcement. Such human utterances as questions, requests, and the like are examples of mands. Another operant, the *tact*, is most closely related to its stimulus. A tact is an utterance that is conditioned by reinforcement during occurrence with a particular object or event (or a property of an object or event) as a stimulus. That a child has been conditioned to utter "ball" when a ball is the stimulis is an example of tact conditioning.

Verbally stimulated operants. Some types of operants are considered to be linked not to direct reinforcement or need states but to other verbal behaviors. For example, an *echoic* operant exists where the behavior is a response to a sound pattern approximating an acoustic stimulus, as for example, where a child tends to reproduce an utterance that he has just heard. A *textual* operant occurs when the response is under the control of some nonauditory verbal stimulus as might be found when one reads aloud in response to the printed word. Another type of functional behavior, called *intraverbal operants*, exists where one part of a verbal stimulus within the individual prompts another one, as in the way saying "Washington" may be a stimulus to an intraverbal response in saying "D.C."

Operant combinations. If we were to consider verbal behavior solely in terms of such basic operants as those described above, we would not be able to explain much of the verbal behavior that we witness in our everyday lives. It is difficult, indeed, to conceive of any but very rudimentary situations of verbal behavior when an utterance could be adequately explained in terms of a single operant. It is important, then, to realize that operants are only the "raw material out of which sustained verbal behavior is manufactured" (Skinner, 1957, p. 312).

In Skinner's theory, the role of the speaker emerges when we consider him as the nucleus of a situation involving the complex interaction among stimulus variables, listener variables, and his own conditioning history. In brief, then, although Skinner places a good deal of emphasis upon the single operants, he is assuming that these are only the ingredients that eventually combine in situations of real verbal behavior.

The individual's role as the locus for the complex combination of operants is discussed by Skinner in a number of ways. For one thing, there is the presumption that most verbal behavior comes under situations of multiple-causation. That is, as a person talks, his production behavior represents the response to multiple controlling stimuli or causes. Some of these causes could include self-stimulation taking place entirely within the speaker's behavior, as in one utterance stimulating another.

Another type of self-stimulation described by Skinner comes under the heading of *autoclitics*. Autoclitics represent a relation between the state (or circumstance) of the speaker and his verbal behavior. If, for example, a person were to say *"I don't think* that ducks have feathers," the italicized part of this statement is considered to be a reflection of the state of the speaker. Sometimes mands serve in autoclitics, such as in the statement "Believe me, all ducks have feathers." Some autoclitics serve in qualification or quantification—for example: "This *is not a* feathered duck", *"All* ducks have feathers."

The Behaviorist Viewpoint: General Considerations

In sum, Skinner's picture depicts the language user within a framework where verbal behavior is explained in terms of controlling stimuli and conditioned responses. There is no attempt to characterize any of the inner processes of the language user, save to assume that the speaker is the coordinating agent capable of responding in a predictable way to multiple causation. Verbal behavior within this framework as seen by Skinner is functional in the sense that it is an effect for which there has been a cause. The aim of Skinner's functional analysis is to identify these cause-effect relations that involve verbal behavior. It is this type of identification that underlies the operants defined in Skinner's theorizing. Obviously, this type of description does not place much stress upon what linguists define in terms of linguistic phenomena. The concepts of phonology, morphology, and syntax, although occasionally mentioned by Skinner, have no major role within his theory.

It is the paucity of linguistic insight that has led to most of the major criticism of Skinner's theory. The landmark among such criticism is the essay-review of *Verbal Behavior* by Noam Chomsky (1959). Although Chomsky indicts all of behavioristic psychology in this essay, one of his particular criticisms of Skinner is that little if anything within his theory took advantage of, or even bore upon, what linguists have been able to tell us about the nature of language. As we shall see, the psycholinguists who are stimulated by Chomsky's linguistic theorizing, have typically used the behavioristic view of language as an argument that new and different theorizing was needed. We shall see some of this under the description of the "cognitive" approach to studying the language user.

On the other hand, because operant conditioning lends itself to operational definition under laboratory conditions, it has had wide use (and acceptance) as a framework or paradigm for researching conditions of verbal learning. For example, there are numerous studies where operant conditioning has been employed to add to, or to extinguish, particular verbal behaviors in people's repertoires. Perhaps the best illustration of these has been the extensive use of the operant conditioning framework in studies with the mentally retarded. Here simple utterances such as naming, a ball, for example, are taught to a subject in an operant conditioning framework. The procedure involves first the conditioning of an echoic operant, then, given the subject's capability to pronounce the word, this emission is next conditioned with the presence of the object itself (as a tact operant). Although such studies do not represent the bulk of the application of Skinner's theorizing, they represent practical aspects of its application (see Spradlin, 1968). This application also illustrates an aspect of behavioristic theory that few people have argued with—that certain aspects of verbal behavior can be added, extinguished, or modified through the use of reinforcement schedules. Thus the Skinnerian framework for operant conditioning has provided a useful definition for such circumstances of conditioning, as well as the definitions of the types of verbal behavior that may be the goals of conditioning within this framework. Whether or not one agrees with Skinner's theorizing, it is still important to know the basis of his reasoning and his terminology in order to understand the contemporary research literature that incorporates a behavioristic view.

Osgood's Mediational Theory

Background

As we said earlier, the main distinction between a strictly behaviorist theory and a mediational theory of the language user is that the latter incorporates some speculation on the types of internal behaviors which lead to the organism's responses. As depicted earlier in figure 5.1, we can consider mediational behaviors as those behaviors which incorporate a stimulus-response sequence *within* the organism. An example of a mediational approach to theorizing about the language user is found in the work of Osgood (1963). In general, Osgood speculates that the internal, mediating, behavior of the organism could take place on any one of, or a combination of, three levels. One of these levels is identified as "reflex" action, such as the behavior that links your sensation of pain from touching a hot stove with jerking your hand away from the stove. Another type of linkage is thought to be the consequence of highly learned stimulus-response relationships, as when somebody yells "Duck! " at you and you do just that. These are the types of internal behaviors that had to be learned, but which we do not stop to "think about" when we perform them. Finally, Osgood conceives of a third level that is akin to "meaning" processes, such as when the organism responds to stimuli which "stand for" other stimuli. It is this level of mediational behavior that Osgood thinks most important to an explanation of how the organism is capable of associating meanings with verbal stimuli. This type of *sign-behavior* is proposed within a theory called the *representational-mediation hypothesis*. We will look at this hypothesis in some detail.

Representational-Mediation Hypothesis

Two-step model. Osgood's hypothesis generally fits within a concept of two-step learning as contrasted with a one-step model such as was seen in Skinner's theory. By two-step we mean that there is a relationship between an overt (external) stimulus and a covert (internal) response in the organism, and there is a further relationship between this covert response and an overt response which the organism could eventually make. Accordingly, if we look at the overall relation between the initial overt stimulus and the final overt response, we have gone through two steps in the mediational behavior. The bulk of Osgood's theorizing in the representational-mediation hypothesis represents an attempt to explain these internal steps.

Constituents of sign-behavior. Figure 5.3 illustrates the major constituents involved in Osgood's representational-mediation hypothesis. Consider for purposes of illustration that $\dot{S}$ is a piece of apple

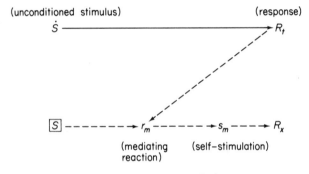

Figure 5.3   Representation-mediation process.

pie and R_t is your response upon perceiving the pie. The $\dot{S}$ and R_t again refer to a stimulus and response relation. The subscripted R_t refers to the total response hierarchy that you would have to that stimulus— for example, recognizing the pie as something to eat, liking it, having your mouth water, having a predisposition to take the pie and eat it, and so on. We would say that $\dot{S}$ is a stimulus (significate) that regularly and reliably elicits a pattern of total response behavior, R_t.

Let us next suppose that a potential verbal stimulus such as the spoken word "pie," is presented and repeated under learning conditions with $\dot{S}$ such that it becomes a stimulus which elicits a response similar to that elicited by $\dot{S}$. Here the spoken word "pie," or $\boxed{S}$, comes to elicit a behavior that is similar to behavior elicited by the pie itself. However, a key point in Osgood's theory is that the response to $\boxed{S}$, that is R_x, is only a portion of the response (R_t) to the original stimulus $(\dot{S})$. In simple terms, $\boxed{S}$ comes to elicit a portion of the original response. Osgood speculates that when $\boxed{S} \rightarrow R_x$ becomes associated with $\dot{S} \rightarrow R_t$ the conditioning which serves the mediating role for the symbolizing process is the relationship between R_t and r_m (mediating reaction), as shown by the diagonal arrow in figure 5.3. That is, during the conditioning process the organism comes to internalize some portion of the R_t behavior, and this is designated as r_m. It is this internal portion, r_m, which has been "detached" from R_t which serves as a basis for the symbolizing process. Internally, r_m is capable of self-stimulating the organism which can lead to a response (R_x); this is the overt-response stage of the process. R_x is a response to the meaning $(r_m \rightarrow s_m)$ of pie, not to a pie itself. The process shown in figure 5.3 is taken by Osgood as a diagram of *sign-behavior*, where $\boxed{S}$ is the sign which can initiate mediating behavior (r_m) which is the basis for the symbolizing process. Osgood, (1963, p. 740), offers a concise description of the process pictured in figure 5.3:

> Whenever some originally neutral stimulus (sign-to-be) $\boxed{S}$, is repeated contiguous with another stimulus (significate), $\dot{S}$, which regularly and reliably elicits a particular pattern of total behavior, R_t, the neutral stimulus will become associated with some portion, r_m, of this total behavior as a representation-mediation process.

Three-Stage Mediation-Integration Model

As we said earlier, Osgood conceives of three types of linkages which could stand between stimulus and response in the organism. His three-stage mediation-integration model is an attempt to combine the representation-mediation process with an overall model which takes into account the two other types of linkages, which he sees playing a role themselves in verbal behavior.

Levels of internal linkages. Figure 5.4 outlines the three-stage model. Note first how the model can be divided into major parts—the three types of internal linkages, such as *reflex*, *automatisms*, and *representation-mediation*, are located in the *projection*, *integrational*, and *representational* levels of the overall model. Consider,

PROCESSES

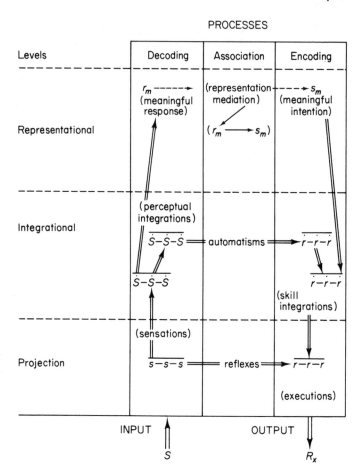

Figure 5.4   Three stage mediation-integration model (from Charles
E. Osgood, "On Understanding and Creating Sentences," *American
Psychologist,* 18, (1963): 740. Reprinted by permission.)

for example, how an input stimulus such as a bright flash of light
might lead to a reflex of iris closure or blinking. All of this would
take place solely on the projection level of this model. By contrast,
consider how hearing your name represents, first, on the input side,
the reflex response of the auditory mechanism, which in turn
stimulates a perceptual recognition, and this might cause you to
look in the direction of the speaker and perhaps utter, "huh?"

or "yes?" Such a sequence of events would involve both the projection and integrational levels, with the linkage (automatism) on the latter level.

Finally, Osgood conceives that when behavior involves the representation level, the input stimuli would typically come through the projection and integration levels to the representation level (r_m). Then self-stimulating behavior (s_m) is capable of setting up a chain of events that activates the three levels of the output side of the model.

Coding and association. The differentiations between input and output processes in the model are identified in the overall labels *decoding* (input side), and *encoding* (output side). Potentially connecting any stage of the decoding and encoding sides is a particular type of association, such as a reflex type of association on the projection level, high habit-strength learned association on the integration level, and a representation-mediation linkage on the representation level.

A Mediational Account of Sentence Behavior

Osgood's theorizing on sentence behavior represents an attempt to explain linguistic details within the framework of his three-stage mediational model. His speculations on sentence processing in encoding and decoding provide an illustration of this.

Expression and content. Like the descriptive linguist, Osgood employs a distinction between the expression and content systems of language. He speculates that a language user's knowledge of the content system is accommodated by learning in the representation-mediation process. That is, meaning itself is considered to be acquired as a representation-mediation process. Relations between this knowledge of content and knowledge of expression, according to Osgood, are found in the learned relationship between perceptual integrations of expression and corollary meaningful responses on the decoding side of the model, as well as between meaningful intentions and linguistic skill integrations on the encoding side of the model. He assumes that the knowledge of the expression system is acquired by the user as perceptual and articulatory habits. On the decoding side, this is the assumption that stimulation of the auditory mechanism and the neural signals that are transmitted to the brain have a conditioned relationship with what we eventually recognize as linguistic expression (perceptual integrations). Or on the encoding side, it is saying that in the creation of an utterance, the neural patterns stimulated by meaningful intentions are patterns (or skill integrations) that lead to the learned-operations of the speech articulators (executions).

In a broad sense, then, Osgood speculates that when we respond to a sentence we are responding first in terms of a series of neural sequences which represent the perception of the expression system. Subsequently, in the higher level representation-mediation processes, such perceptions eventually give way to our conscious recognition of the meaning of an utterance. In creating an utterance, content gives way to a series of events stimulating the expression system into eventual articulatory behavior.

Linguistic identifications. Osgood has attempted to identify some of the details of language with the processes in his mediational model. On the decoding side of the projection level, for example, he speculates that the distinctive features (Chapter 3) in the speech sequence define the significant pattern of an input stimulus. That is, of all of the phenomena in the acoustic wave, it is the distintive features of speech sounds that constitute the key initial input. Osgood further speculates that responses to these distinctive features (as neural signals on the integration level) lead to our recognition of phonemes in the expression system and are eventually structured in our perceptions into the recognition of words as expressive units.

One of Osgood's key proposals is that as words are recognized as integral expressive units, the perception of expression gives way to the perception of content. It is the word that serves on the borderline between the perception processes which involve the recognition of the details of linguistic expression and the recognition of particular meanings.

Beginning at the level of word meanings, Osgood further speculates that the syntactic patterns perceived along with words provide a guide for the structuring of word meanings into phrase meanings and eventually sentence meanings. As we decode from the word level on, we are structuring the content of words into the content of phrases and sentences (and eventually messages).

Osgood proposes a somewhat opposite sequence in encoding, where the initial creation of an utterance began as an intended meaning. As this intended meaning is encoded into a linguistic form at the word level, it becomes a process involving the structuring of expression rather than of meaning. On the integration level, according to Osgood, this encoding or structuring of expression is initially relevant to speech as potential syllable production, and this eventually gives way to the production of the distinctive features by the speech articulators.

Mediational Viewpoint: General Considerations

In overview, it is useful to remember that Osgood's theory simply represents an attempt to provide an account of those types of internal behaviors which may intervene between the stimulation of the organism and its response. This essentially is "filling in" of the box shown earlier between stimulus and response in figure 5.1. A particularly ambitious portion of Osgood's theorizing is the attempt to account for meaning as a sign-type of response (r_m) which is an internalized increment of some original response (R_t), then to incorporate this process within a hierarchy of mediational processes to account for language behavior.

As compared with the behavioristic account, the great challenge of the mediational account comes in verification. How is it possible to test this model in terms of what it hypothesizes? Ideally, and as Osgood occasionally suggests, the best verification of this model would be the eventual discovery of its physiologic basis in neural behavior. But since such an ideal may be a long time coming, or may never be totally possible, the mediational psychologist typically looks for observable evidence outside the organism that has implications regarding the operation of internal processes. This approach has been described by an analogy of the mind as a closed box, the inside of which we will never see, but which has strings leading in one side and a related set of strings leading out in the opposite direction. By seeing how the manipulation of strings on one side affects the movement of strings on the opposite side, one would eventually be able to deduce a system of levers or pulleys that might operate within the box. What this crude analogy says to us is that by the careful examination of the relationships between stimulating conditions of verbal behavior and responses to those stimulating conditions, we should be able to accumulate evidence which would either point to the integrity of the proposed model, or suggest some alternatives.

Probably the best known application of Osgood's representation-mediation hypothesis is its role as the theoretical underpinning of a scaling instrument known as the *semantic differential*. Some research in use of the semantic differential has reinforced speculations of how meaning behavior, particularly connotative behavior, may operate. However, this has shed little light upon the sentence processing speculations which we have discussed.

Familarity with Osgood's theorizing has also come as a result of a test known as the *Illinois Test of Psycholinguistic Abilities*. The subparts of this test attempt to measure behaviors that are presumed to be symptomatic of capabilities on the projection, integration, and representational levels. As some critics have complained (Severson and Guest, 1970), the use and assumptions of this test have far exceeded the theory upon which it is based.

The Cognitive View

Background

As we said earlier, the cognitive viewpoint places no stress upon the stimulus-response aspects of language behavior, save to recognize that language could exist within such situations. Instead, this approach focuses upon what a language user *would have to know* and what he *would have to do* in order to create and to understand sentences in his language. Most of the beginnings of the current cognitive viewpoint can be dated in the early 1960s when the linguist, Chomsky (see esp., 1959) and the psycholinguist, Miller (1962, 1965) published indictments of the behavioristic and mediational accounts of language behavior. Some of the early contributions to the formulation of a cognitive viewpoint have also come from Lenneberg's (1967) speculations on the type of a biological endowment that a language user appears to have.

Preliminaries to the Cognitive Viewpoint

One of the best summary arguments of the shortcomings of the learning theory accounts of language behavior was given by Miller (1965). Some of his key points are discussed next.

Phonemitization. One inadequacy of learning theory approaches is in accounting for the concept of *phonemitization* in language acquisition and language behavior. As can be seen in Chapters 2 and 3 only a relatively small portion of the acoustic characteristics of a speech wave are pertinent to language. Generally, the linguistically significant acoustic characteristics, whether viewed relative to distinctive features or phonemes, require that the language user be able to sort them out from all else in the speech wave. The key question is: Why and how does the language user learn to recognize these particular acoustic aspects and not others? If this acquisition is explained in terms of a learning theory model, the answer would require that the young child be able to detect and to learn very fine discriminations in the speech wave. This also requires that he be able to sense that he has been reinforced for recognizing or using the "correct" discriminations. Such an explanation would require a great amount of linguistic experience on the part of the child. Moreover, all of this experience would have to occur under appropriate conditions of reinforcement. Somehow, as a part of the process of language acquisition, the human is capable of acquiring or developing a phonemic system for the language of his speech community/ Most learning theories would account for child's acquisition of phonemitization ability in much the same way that a parrot can learn to imitate the sound configurations of some words of a language. The key difference, however, between the parrot and the child is revealed when we find that the parrot, if learning a new and different "language" would have no accent. That is, he would have no carryover of a phoneme system, whereas the child would. Humans are uniquely capable of phonemitization, and learning theories do not offer an adequate account for this.

Reference as against meaning. Another shortcoming of learning theory explanations is the inadequacy of their accounting for the difference between reference and meaning in verbal behavior. As Miller (1965) pointed out, the utterances "George Washington," "The first President of the United States," and "The General of the American Revolutionary Armies" all *refer* to the same person. But we do recognize several distinctions in terms of the meanings of these three utterances. The problem illustrated here is that most learning theory approaches to language behavior, if they even attempt to account for meaning, show it as a relationship between expression and reference. The question then is: How does one learn to make the discriminations among meanings which have generally the same referent? An implication of this question is that meaning in language must be built upon something beyond simple reference. We add to the problem when we attempt to account for the meanings of words which have no physical reference. How, for example, can we account for the meaning of "democracy"?

Linguistic experience. One of the most challenging arguments raised by Miller is that even if we take a relatively generous view of how much experience a child would have to have in order to witness the utterances that he is capable of making at the age of, say, five years, he would have to have lived something like a 1000 times the estimated age of the earth!

The Competence-Performance Dichotomy

As for the question, What is it the user uses when he uses language? Chomsky has argued that the concept of linguistic *competence* provides a starting point for an answer. As we described in Chapter 4, a generative grammar represents the attempt to state linguistic knowledge (or *competence*) in terms of the rules that an ideal speaker-listener would have for the creation and understanding of utterances. Chomsky has proposed that his theory of linguistic competence is a basis for hypothesizing about the nature of the actual linguistic knowledge held by actual speaker-listeners. However, there have been some misunderstandings of Chomsky's statements in the area, generally in that Chomsky's model of linguistic knowledge has been offered as a direct psychological model. Such is not the case; Chomsky has advised that the psycholinguist, or the researcher into language *performance*, should have as his goal the separate development of a psychological model. Speculations on the nature of the psychological model would benefit from implications drawn from the more abstract model of linguistic competence. Also the psychological model should eventually incorporate a performance account of linguistic knowledge, its behavioral nature, acquisition, and use. Some of Miller and Chomsky's early but detailed thinking on performance models have been published elsewhere (1963).

Biological Endowment

/*Linguistic universals.* Another implication in theorizing about linguistic competency is the existence of characteristics that are universal to grammars of all languages. These include, for example, the relevance of distinctive feature phonological classifications to all languages, the universality of certain types of phrase structure and transformational rules, the applicability of phonological, syntactic, and semantic components, and so on. As for phonological universals, the performance implication is that man uses the speech sounds he does mainly because he is biologically "programmed" for them, both in terms of recognition and production. Thus while we might say that the ability for phonemitization is biologically endowed, the phonology of a *particular* language is what must be developed. Obviously, such thinking greatly reshapes the types of questions asked in research on language development./

/Regarding biological endowment per se, Lenneberg (1967) cites examples of how language or language-like skills develop in children who have severe pathologies, both in terms of deafness, inabilities to articulate, and even cases of relatively severe mental retardation. Lenneberg has asserted that this development is evidence of the human propensity for developing language skills. Similarly he cites a number of cases where severe environmental deprivation surrounded a child's development, but where language or language-like behavior still emerged./

One of the major arguments in favor of a biological component is that many of the stages of language development can be seen to correlate with biophysical aspects of human development, particularly with certain indices of brain maturation. Lenneberg has argued that the stages of language acquisition may follow a biologically defined, maturational timetable. It is the environment, Lenneberg thinks, which eventually determines what a child learns at a particular level of development and the extent of learning at each level, but it is the biological component that sets the timetable and stages for this.

New Research Priorities

The foregoing considerations of the nature of the language user not only present a rather drastic shift from learning theory accounts, but indeed change the type of questions that are asked about the psychology of the language user. Foremost among these are: (1) What is the psychological nature of linguistic knowledge? (2) Which linguistic capabilities are biologically endowed? (3) Given biological endowment, what then has to be learned about language? (4) Given linguistic knowledge, what are the processes of employing it in sentence creation and understanding?

We will next view some of the ideas for researching answers to these questions, all of which will reflect the concerns of the cognitive viewpoint.

Derivational Complexity Studies

Rationale. As described earlier, one of the ways of drawing upon the theory of linguistic competence in the formulation of a theory of linguistic performance was to look for evidence of particular types of competence in actual situations of verbal performance. Most of the early studies which were prompted by this strategy involved experiments whereby persons were subjected to a verbal behavior task which presumably involved the use of specific linguistic rules. The objective was to see whether some of the characteristics of these linguistic rules would yield expected manifestations in behavior. One relatively simple thesis which underlay many of the early studies was that the more linguistic rules that a user would have to use in a given situation, the greater would be the demands upon his language-processing behavior. By observing the times necessary for task accomplishment, by observing errors, or other indicies, it was presumed that these demands could be revealed in experiments. Studies along this line have been identified under the label of the *derivational theory of complexity*.

Figure 5.5 illustrates one of the bases for a number of studies testing the complexity thesis. In generative grammar, it was initially proposed that underlying all sentences of a language is a set of basic or underlying sentences. These were called *kernel* (*K*) sentences and had an active-affirmative form (as in: "Bill hit the ball."). Kernel sentences were accounted for by phrase structure rules, which characterized their "derivational history" or "deep structure." [Recall in Chapter 4, pp. 67–71, that phrase structure rules (PS) accounted for the deep structure of an utterance, whereas transformational (T) rules accounted for variations in the surface sequence.] A speculation about a psychological performance model was that kernel sentences could represent the input into surface transformations. In early versions of the grammar, the passive (P), passive-negative (PN), and negative (N) forms were derived by such transformations. A performance hypothesis stemming from these interrelations was that if one were to perform

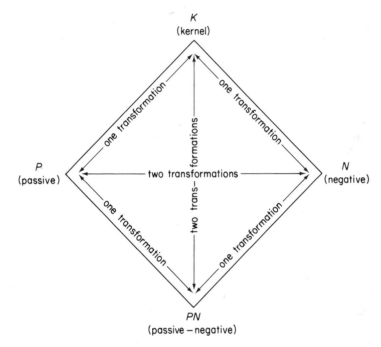

Figure 5.5 Derivational complexity diagram.

tasks which involved going from a K form of a sentence to a P form, or from a K form to a PN form, that the more surface transformations this involved, the more demand it would impose upon performance. One measure of demands was the time taken for transformations. Figure 5.5 shows the number of transformations separating the four forms. It was hypothesized that the generation of a PN sentence would take more time than a P sentence, which in turn took more time than a K sentence. An intriguing question was whether the time taken to create a P sentence from a K sentence plus the time taken to create a PN sentence from a P sentence would equal the total amount of time to go straight from the K to the PN form. This would imply that sentence transformation rules representing these forms had psychological reality, or at least something akin to serial use of rules was involved in their performance.

Such theorizing took no account as to the detailed psychological nature of the transformation rule but only assumed that somehow in the language user's capabilities the relationship among these simple sentence forms could be accounted for by performance of transformational steps. A variety of studies along this or closely related lines was undertaken.

Some sample studies. In an early paper, Miller (1962) summarized some ongoing and as yet incomplete research which involved a task where persons were supposed to find matchings of the "same" sentences as they appeared on two lists but in different transformational forms (see Fig. 5.5). On one list the sentence might be passive (P), as in "The ball was hit by Bill." On the other list it was negative (N), as in "Bill did not hit the ball." Again, the task was to find the sentences on separate lists that had the same subjects and objects. By mixing together sentences on both lists that varied in terms of different transformations, it was eventually possible to calculate the average amount of time for a subject to match, for example, a K (kernel) form with a N (negative) form, or a N form with a PN (passive-negative) form, and the like. Preliminary evidence reported by Miller (1962) revealed that it would generally take longer to match sentences separated by two surface transformations (e.g., K and PN) than sentences which varied by only one surface transformation (K and P, P and PN, etc., as in Fig. 5.5). This initial research evidence which suggested the psychological reality of transformational rules stimulated a host of studies of this type. In a later paper, however, Miller and McKean (1964) published a time study involving the matching of simple sentences, but here the results were somewhat ambiguous as to whether time differences were actually supportive of transformational rule processing. In brief, this later report cast doubt on the implications of the earlier study.

Another early study that attracted substantial attention and illustrates the derivational complexity thesis was one of simple sentence learning conducted by Mehler (1963). He had persons attempt to learn a variety of sentences of different transformational types, with the expectation that those sentences which were the least transformationally complex would be the easiest learned (i.e., fastest learned, fewest errors). Generally Mehler's results indicated that the K form sentence was the easiest learned of a variety of different types of sentence transformations. However, an intriguing bit of evidence pointing toward a refinement of the derivational complexity thesis was found in the types of errors that persons made when they incorrectly recalled transformationally complex sentences. Generally such errors were that if a sentence, say of the PN form, were incorrectly recalled, the error was often one reflecting a "loss" of one of the original transformations. Sometimes a PN or N sentence, for example, was recalled only in a K form. A speculation was that when persons stored transformed sentences in memory, they were somehow storing the K form of the sentence along with the "tag" which would indicate a transformation or transformations of a particular type. This was a psychological thesis that at the time fit quite closely with the notion that the K form underlay all surface forms of sentences. Thus the implication was that when a person perceived a transformationally complex sentence he would be "untransforming" it down to its K form and then interpreting that K form along with whatever transformational tags might be indicated. Similarly if he were to recall that sentence, or again utter it as a part of a recall task, he would have to then transform (recode) the K form according to the "tags" indicating its original complex form. This was called the *recoding* hypothesis. Although Mehler's speculations were in line with the derivational complexity thesis, it should be noted that these were only speculations, and not something that was directly tested in his study.

Probably one of the most imaginative studies which followed from Mehler's notion of a recoding hypothesis was an investigation conducted by Savin and Perchonock (1965). Like Mehler's study, this involved a task where persons tried to learn sentences which varied in transformational complexity. Pursuing the "tag" thesis, Savin and Perchonock reasoned that if a person was to recall a sentence which had, say, two transformations (e.g., PN) this should take more space in his temporary memory than say the recall of a sentence with only one transformation (P), and that would take more than a sentence which contained no transformations (e.g., K). Savin and Perchonock's reasoning was that each one of the transformational tags should take up space in temporary memory. Their way of measuring this amount of space in the learning and recall task was to have persons try to remember extra words along with each sentence. Presumably the more space that would be taken in memory by the recall of a sentence and its transformational tags, the fewer words (in addition to the sentence) a person could recall. Thus it was expected that if their "space" thesis obtained, a person recalling the most transformationally complex sentences would recall the fewest additional words; or recalling a less complex sentence would result in more words recalled, and so on. Savin and Perchonock's results were persuasively supportive of the thesis. Unfortunately, however, attempts to replicate these results have been unsuccessful and researchers have also given alternative interpretations of the results. Hence, there are serious reservations whether the study actually supports the derivational theory of complexity.

Arguments against the thesis. Beyond the details of the above studies, the important point is that the relatively early psychological studies which reflected the cognitive approach were in one way or another attempting to find evidence of the psychological reality of individual transformational rules. Given the relatively powerful description of rules provided by a generative grammar, it seemed reasonable to search in the behavior of the language user for psychological evidence of such rules. Generally, however, such studies have led to equivocable results, and they eventually became generally disfavored as reflected in papers by Fodor and Garrett (1966, 1967). These critics admonished psycholinguistic researchers for their assumptions that the *details* of grammatical behavioral processes would necessarily follow the details of grammatical rules. An analogy here was that grammatical rules imply no more about their behavioral correlates than mathematical rules explain about how our mind works when we add two-plus-two.

Fodor and Garrett argued that the only assumption one could make in researching the cognitive view was that language behavior involved the processing of sentences from a *deep* structural form (as they exist in the mind) to a *surface* form (as they are articulated or heard). Generative grammar may provide us with implications about these processes, but according to Fodor and Garrett, seeking psychological evidence of individual grammatical rules may be assuming too close a fit between the grammar and its details of performance.

In a series of experiments, Fodor and Garrett (1967)

attempted to illustrate that: (1) Sentence comprehension involves the language user's heuristics (discovery procedures) in inducing deep structure from clues in surface structure, rather than the operation of grammatical rules; (2) Differences in sentence performance are a function of the degree to which the elements and their arrangements in surface structure provide clues to the elements and relations in deep structure, rather than the number of transformational rules which separate the levels. A brief description of several of the experiments illustrates the meanings of the above concepts as well as providing an example of the type of psycholinguistic research that succeeded the derivational complexity studies.

Fodor and Garrett (1967) reasoned that relative pronouns in self-embedded sentences, such as "The man *whom* the dog bit died," provide a surface structure clue as to deep structure relationships. Here this relationship is that of the sentential patterns of "man died" and "dog bit man." Presumably, "whom" helps to clarify that man is the subject of one sentence and the object of another. Without the relative pronoun the sentence is still grammatical but may be more difficult to understand: "The man the dog bit died." This difficulty is magnified even more in sentences having two embedded clauses:

> The tiger the lion the gorilla chased killed was ferocious.

> (compared with)

> The tiger which the lion that the gorilla chased killed was ferocious.

In one experiment, the researchers had persons attempt to restate such sentences immediately after hearing them. Responses were scored in terms of latency (how soon the restatement was given) and in terms of the number of subject-object relations which were correctly restated. As predicted, persons were better able to restate sentences containing relative pronouns than those without them. Although this finding was supportive of the idea that the relative pronouns served as surface feature clues of deep structural relations, several alternative explanations could be offered. One was that the pronouns simply gave the subjects a kind of "break" between the sentence segments and thus facilitated their perception of the individual units. However, in a second experiment brief segments of blank tape inserted between the segments (in place of pronouns) did not serve to increase the rate of correct restatements over the pronoun-less versions. This denied the alternative explanation concerning segmentation.

Another alternative explanation was that subtle intonation features in the two readings of the sentences for the first experiment could have contributed to the differences. This alternative was denied in a third experiment where the sentences were recorded in a highly expressive manner. But adding these maximal intonation features did not change the difference in restatement of the pronoun and pronoun-less sentence sets.

Still another alternative explanation was a return to the derivational complexity theory—that the pronoun-less versions were more difficult because the difference between them and the pronoun versions are accounted for by an added transformation. That is, a pronoun-less version represents the addition of a transformation rule to explain the deletion of each pronoun. This explanation was countered by an experiment where adjectives were added to the pronoun-less sentences—for example, "The *first* shot the *tired* soldier the mosquito bit fired missed." Accounting for these additions adds six transformations in contrast with the original pronoun-less version, and eight as compared with the pronoun version. If complexity of performance were predicted from transformational complexity, then one would expect the adjective versions of the pronoun-less sentences to be by far the most difficult of all versions to restate accurately. Such was not the case; in fact, the adjective versions were slightly better in restatement scores than the pronoun-less versions without the adjectives. In short, predictions from the derivational complexity theory were not supported in the results. Instead, the adjectives were interpreted as themselves serving as clues to the deep structure relations of the sentence.

In all, the above experiments illustrate the trend in psycholinguistic investigation to the question of perceptual strategies in sentence comprehension. Presumably, the language user develops procedures whereby he can estimate deep structures from clues perceived in surface structures. It seems that these strategies are not the operation of grammatical rules as hypothesized in derivational complexity theory, but are simply perceptual behaviors. Only the consequences of these strategies might be described by grammatical rules, not the strategies themselves.

Language Development

Perhaps the best known theoretical extension of the cognitive view to the study of the linguistic development of a child is in the work of McNeill (especially, 1970). Following the Chomskian view, McNeill assumes that as a child develops language, he is acquiring linguistic knowledge, or *competence*. Again such competence should be describable in terms of a system of linguistic rules. Whereas many of the best known studies of language acquisition have typically been inventories of the sounds, words, or phrases that children at one age or another were capable of saying, McNeill has argued that we can only understand the development of performance capabilities in the child when we have understood the nature of the development of competence. The first question, then, is: How can we describe the development of competence? A second is: How can we describe the processes by which a child's performance with language derives from such competence?

Taking a largely nativist view of language development, McNeill, like Lenneberg, assumes that the child comes biologically predisposed to develop language. Also, following ideas posed by Chomsky, McNeill speculates that a key facet of this predisposition is the child's capability for inducing from a finite amount of linguistic experience a finite set of linguistic rules (competency). This finite competency underlies a capability of creating and understanding (performing) a theoretically infinite variety of utterances. Most of McNeill's speculation beyond this point has been an attempt to describe the kind of competency that a child has at various stages of language development, particularly in the very early stages of syntactic development. In an early major essay, McNeill (1966), while surveying the relatively rudimentary syntactic structures found in the speech of children, attempted to write grammatical rules which might characterize the competence needed to create and understand these utterances.

One main example among this type of theorizing was in how the child could be seen to use an early type of modification pattern, involving a pivot class word (e.g., *big*) as against an open class word (e.g., *boat*). The type of rule proposed to account for such modification by the child was as follows:

$$S \rightarrow (P) + O$$

Here "*S*" stood for the syntactic construction, ' (*P*)" for the option of a pivot class word, and "*O*" for the open class word. Consider the combinations that could be made by combining one *P* and one *O* word, or else using only a single *O* word, from the list below (compiled from McNeill, 1966):

Pivot Class	*Open Class*
big	boy
my	sock
pretty	fan
Daddy	shoe
	hot
	Daddy

Although it is difficult to prove that the child is actually exercising a $S \rightarrow (P) + O$ rule, this is a way to describe syntactic patterning of his utterances. More generally the rule says that we can expect to find *O* class words occurring alone or in the $P + O$ combination. We would not expect to find *P* class words occurring alone, unless they involve words that are in both pivot and open class categories. The attractiveness of such rules lies in that a description of the development of linguistic competence, as contrasted with copious inventories of performance, is a much more economical way to describe the development of language capabilities in the child.

On the other hand, there is the question whether adult researchers can be sure of their interpretation of the syntactic patterns underlying the child's utterances. Bloom (1970), for example, in carefully assessing utterances relative to contextual factors, found that grammatical interpretations of children's structures were sometimes different from what might be superficially assumed. Thus, for example, an utterance such as "Daddy shoe" may not be an approximation to the adult adjective + noun rule for modification, but may be an approximation to a subject + predicate construction ("Daddy gets the shoe").

In all such research of this type there is usually an attempt to see how the child's rules develop as increasing approximations to adult grammar. One application of this line of reasoning is to consider how in child-and-adult conversations there may be a give-and-take between their grammatical competencies. An early study in this area was reported in a well-known paper by Brown and

Bellugi (1964) concerning processes in the child's acquisition of syntax.

After observing the verbal interaction of a young boy and girl with their parents, Brown and Bellugi speculated that there seemed to be at least three processes pertinent to the acquisition of syntax. One of these, called *imitation with reduction*, is when a child paraphrases an adult utterance but reduces it to a simplified grammar. Such an example would be: *Parent:* "Mommy is having her eggnog now." *Child:* "Mommy eggnog." Another process, called *imitation with expansion*, comes when an adult paraphrases a child's utterance but expands it according to an adult grammar. An example of this would be: *Child:* "My toy." *Parent:* "This is baby's toy." It was the expansion and reduction interplay between parent and child that led Brown and Bellugi to speculate that a child induced from such experience the generative rules which eventually allowed him to create adult-like utterances. Thus they defined the third process as *induction of latent structure*.

／Some experimental research has been conducted where groups of children have been exposed to different types of adult-child verbal interactions, and the children compared for relative progress in language development. In one such study, Cazden (1965) in daily half-hour sessions over a three month period gave children in one group expansions (e.g., "Daddy shoe" expanded to "This is daddy's shoe"), and the children in another group a conversational comment (*modelling*) on everything that they said. For example, the child might say, "My dog," then the adult would comment by saying, "Yes, that is your dog and his name is Sparky." Still another group of children received no special verbal treatment. In terms of tests of verbal development, children in the expansion group did slightly better than those who received no treatment, but the children in the modelling group made a large jump in development.／

Needless to say, the area of child language development holds rich topics for research. Beyond simply identifying the experience that a child needs in order to acquire language, there is the deeper question of how he internalizes that experience in the form of linguistic knowledge. Some of the recent research in child language development has been shifted to the very young infant [e.g., Moffitt (1969); McCaffrey (1969)] with the idea that early capabilities for detecting phonological distinctions might hold implications for how a child interprets linguistic experience. Obviously, too, theoretical inquiries into language development cannot be too far removed from considerations of cognitive development. A current view of issues involved in this consideration has been reported by Bever (1970). Granted that a child may come biologically endowed to induce or somehow develop the rules of a language, it is nevertheless important to realize that linguistic experience is, initially at least, essentially phonological. Thus it seems reasonable to assume that a perceptual predisposition for language should be found in children's perception of the phonological features of the language—as in the recognition of distinctive features, intonation patterns, and the like.

The Cognitive View: General Considerations

Although this is a debatable point in some quarters, contemporary psycholinguistic research appears increasingly motivated by the cognitive view. Again, a fundamental distinction in the cognitive view is between competence and performance. The study of actual language behavior, or *performance*, involves a consideration of a variety of factors among which is linguistic knowledge (*competence*). As mentioned earlier, the attractiveness of the cognitive viewpoint is that it attempts to meet the challenge of a psychological theory of the language user that will accommodate the complexities that are known of the nature of language. On the other hand, the frustration with the cognitive viewpoint is the great difficulty that it presents in being susceptable to verification, let alone the arguments that some theorists raise on what the nature of such verification should be (if any at all).

6 | Sociological Perspectives

In Chapter 5 we considered the human capability for creating and understanding utterances. In this chapter we turn to a consideration of how use of this capability is inextricably tied to the contexts of speech, and how these contexts in turn are tied to the social structures and social roles of speaker-listeners.

Sociological Aspects of Linguistic Study

Only in the several contemporary studies to be discussed in this chapter have we had a working partnership between sociology and linguistics. Heretofore there had been sociological aspects of linguistic study but the tools and methods of research were mainly those belonging to the linguist or anthropologist.

The contemporary ideas and research strategies which could most aptly be called sociolinguistic are largely focused *within* speech communities, although generalizations based upon study within communities are susceptible to comparison across communities. These generalizations center upon the study of relations between linguistic variables and such social variables as are characteristic of speech situations, types of speech demanded by different speech situations, and how speakers themselves differ in their performances in meeting these demands. Sociolinguistic study is so new, however, that how these variables are defined and researched varies drastically among theorists and among researchers.

Urban Language Research as an Example
of Sociolinguistic Study

During the 1960s there were several major efforts undertaken in the United States to study relations between language and
social stratification. Here social stratification refers to the combined
difference in income, occupation, and social class of people. In-
vestigations such as those by William Labov (1966) in New York
City and by Roger Shuy and his colleagues (Shuy, Wolfram, and
Riley, 1967) in Detroit represented a working combination of
sociologic and linguistic research methods.

Basic Strategies

Variables.   Most of the variables of sociolinguistic investigation can be identified in the urban language studies. Although
speakers in urban language research have typically been interviewed in a single setting (their home), the researchers manipulated
the speech situations so as to prompt speech varying from informal
to formal in styles. Variation in style is one sociolinguistic variable.
The linguistic features researched in urban language studies have
chiefly been those thought correlated with social stratification—
for example, the pronunciation of /r/ in New York City or the use
of grammatical nonstandardizations such as multiple negation
("I haven't got none.") in Detroit. These features constitute
linguistic variables in sociolinguistic study. The range of variation
(e.g., different usages, pronunciations) of such variables has been
defined as the *linguistic continuum.* Finally, speakers in the urban
language studies have been classified in terms of such social variables as education, occupation, and income, as well as sex and age.
Sampling. In contrast to traditional linguistic field study,
the urban language studies have incorporated a quantitative dimen-
sion. Whereas the linguist often works with one or only a few
informants, the urban researchers have attempted to study groups of
speakers so selected as to be representative of a speaker population.
That is, they have used the *sampling* methods of sociologic studies.
This allows the researcher to use a sample of people in order to
make inferences about a population. The consistency with which a

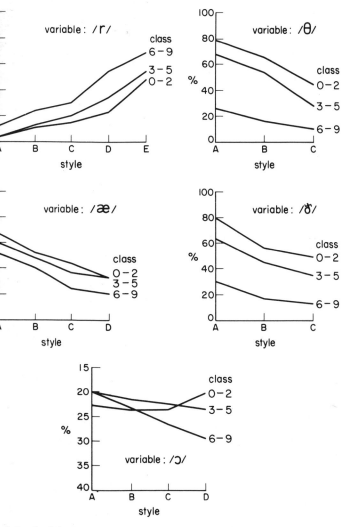

6.1 Social class variations and speech style variation of the
ic variables (from William Labov, *The Social Stratification of English
York City*. Washington, D.C.: Center for Applied Linguistics, 1966.
·d by permission).

variable is found in a specified form in the behavior of a sample of persons gives a basis for making inferences about the population represented by that sample. This basis is in the use of inferential statistics, which provides researchers with an index for gauging the confidence with which they can make inferences about a linguistic variable in a well defined population—for example, inferences about the pronunciation of /r/ by persons living on the lower East side of Manhattan, etc.

Frequency data. Another aspect of quantification has been in studying the frequency with which variations in a linguistic variable are found, as, for example, the relative frequency with which /r/ is pronounced in particular ways, depending upon the speaker and his situation of speaking. Such quantification is in contrast to the descriptive linguist's usual interest in only the qualitative description of a language. In qualitative description, the linguist attempts to abstract from his observations of speech events the most thorough yet simplest description of the language, as in finding the one set of phonemes that could account for the basic sounds of that language.

Recall in Chapter 4 how variation which could not be predicted upon linguistic grounds (as in morphological or phonological conditioning) was left undescribed and considered as *free* or *random* variation. By contrast, sociolinguistic researchers have observed that frequencies of this latter type of variation can often be predicted upon the basis of such variables as the speaker's social status and the formality of the speech situation. We would probably find, for example, that a standard-English-speaking person's full articulation of an "-ing" [ŋ] ending would occur 90 to 100 percent of the time in formal speech situations (e.g., as in job interviews) as compared with something less than this percentage in informal situations (casual, conversational speech) where the incidence of a "in" [-n] allophone typically increases. Here the linguistic variable is the /ŋ/ phoneme; the continuum, the relative incidence of [n] as against [ŋ] realizations; and the situation mainly a differentiation among informal to formal circumstances of speaking.

The speaker. Urban language research has involved the linguistic study of social stratification primarily in the identification of speakers from different socioeconomic strata within city areas. Given this classification of the speaker, linguistic variables which have predictable variations in the speaker's performance in specified situations are identified. The eventual combined description of speaker, linguistic variable, situations, and range of variation (linguistic continuum) comprise the product of a typical urban language study. Some examples will be described next.

Labov's New York Research

Linguistic variables. A substantial part of Labov's (1966) argument for studying New York City speech was that much of its phonological description had either overlooked speakers who used nonstandard forms or had relegated extensive amounts of phonologic variation to the "scrap heap" of random or free variation. Accordingly a major criterion for selecting linguistic variables was that they represented those items heretofore found particularly susceptible to free variation. He further restricted his selection to items that appeared frequently in speech, were thought relatively immune to conscious modification or suppression by the speaker, and could be quantified and interpreted in terms of the larger linguistic system within which they occurred. These main linguistic variables are summarized as follows:

1. The presence or absence of /r/ in final or preconsonantal positions as in such words as "car", "fire", "fired", "beer", "beard", etc.
2. The height of the vowel (generally /æ/) in the words "bad", "bag", "ask", "pass", "cash", and "dance".
3. The realization of the mid-back rounded vowel /ɔ/ as in "caught", "talk", "awed", "dog", "off", "lost", and "all".
4. The variation of [d]-like sounds for the voiced "th" [ð] consonant as in "then" or "that".
5. The variation of [t]-like sounds for the unvoiced "th" [θ] consonant as in "thing" or "think".

Situation variable. Although Labov gathered his data on the above linguistic variables in an interview situation, there was an attempt to vary the situation in such a way as to elicit different

styles of speech. (It is reasonable to assert tha̱ the situation itself.) In summary variations ir

A. Casual speech situation: pri̱ setting as in speech before or a̱ during a break; speech to a p̱ interviewer; speech which rep̱ monologue rather than a specifi̱ question; speech associated wi̱ and customs; and speech wẖ cussing the danger of death.
B. Formal interview situation: the̱ sponses that were typically a sc̱ interview, particularly as the sp̱ his language was being studied.
C. Reading situation: the speech w̱ reading aloud.
D–E. Word lists and minimal pairs:̱ resulted when reading alouḏ words, and when some represeṉ (e.g., "dock-dark", "bared-bad")̱

Speaker classification. In sampling a s̱ Labov sought groups of informants whose langua̱ be taken as representative of portions of the New̱ tion. His guide for sampling was a sociologic stuḏ population several years earlier. In describing̱ important index was social stratification. This wa̱ of a combination of factors of occupation, educa̱ which together enabled Labov to divide his speaḵ ranging from "lower class" to "upper middle clas̱

An example of results. The data of this s̱ variations in three main variables: (1) the lingui̱ their variations (linguistic continuum), (2) the ma̱ speech situation, and (3) the different catego̱ Figure 6.1 illustrates the type of quantitative̱ obtained from the data. These are the results̱ relations between the social class of speakers (0–̱ high), the variations in the speech situation (A̱ performance variations on the five linguistic v̱

lines show a uniform change of values from left to right, this indicates variation according to the range from informal to formal situations (styles). As the lines vary from one another within a given plot, this indicates social class differences in performance.

Shuy's Detroit Research

Speakers. The informants in the Detroit research (Shuy, Wolfram, and Riley, 1967), were a random sample consisting of approximately 700 residents intended to represent specific age, ethnic, and social status groups of Detroit. Social status was classified upon the basis of a combined index incorporating factors of occupation, education, and residence.

Speech situation. Interviews were conducted in the homes of informants where different fieldworkers simultaneously interviewed members of the family. By varying what was asked of informants, the researchers attempted to elicit varying styles of speech, particularly as speech would range from "careful" (formal) to "casual" (informal). This was done by having segments of the interview devoted to free-response conversation on such topics as games and leisure, school, group structure (friends, aspirations, neighborhood, etc.), fighting, accidents, and illness. The interview also involved asking for names of things in and about the house (e.g., variations in what they call the "front room," "living room," "parlor," "sitting room," etc.), having informants read words in isolation as well as continuous context.

Linguistic variables. Because all interviews were tape recorded, the Detroit study provided a wide range of potential types of response data for the identification of linguistic variables. Examples of variables reported upon in the study (Shuy, et al., 1967) are as follows:

> multiple negation ("He can't hit nobody.")
> pronominal apposition ("The other guy, he came in.")
> nasalized vowel allophone (where the realization of a nasal consonant is in the nasalization of a surrounding vowel or semi-vowel rather than the articulation of the consonant).

As an example of the results of the study, figure 6.2 illustrates the correlation between social status of informants and the

percentage incidence of multiple negation. Here the generalization
is that the incidence of multiple negation successively increases from
the upper middle status group to the lower working classgroup.

   Some generalizations. In overview, the urban language
studies by Labov and by Shuy and his colleagues point toward two

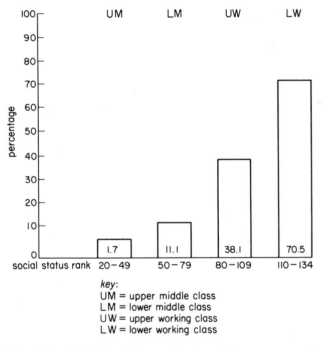

Figure 6.2   Social class differences in the relative percentage of
multiple negation (from Roger W. Shuy, "The Sociolinguists
and Urban Language Problems," in *Language and Poverty:
Perspectives on a Theme*, ed. F. Williams. Chicago: Markham,
1970. Adapted by permission).

main social variables, each identified with linguistic variation.
These are (1) the social class of the speaker and (2) the formality
of his speech situation.

   Although the results given in figures 6.1 and 6.2 show a
definite relation between the speaker's social status or the formality
of the speech situation and particular linguistic usages, it is important to remember that this relation only applies to specific

populations of speakers, specific linguistic variables, and specific speech situations. This close tie to the everyday world of speakers serves to emphasize the highly specific type of description given in sociolinguistic study as compared with the more idealized description provided by traditional linguistic investigation. Whereas the specific or realistic description may be useful in characterizing the detailed behavior of certain speakers in certain situations, it lacks the economy and generality to large groups of speakers that the idealized description provides. In the broadest view, one type of description is really no "better" than the other. Our uses of one or the other depend on our goals.

One of the byproducts of urban language study has been a more objective view of the language behaviors of persons who do not speak the so-called "standard" version of the language. No matter what dialect Americans speak—"Black" or Negro non-standard English in America, "Appalachian", "East Texan", "Bostonian", etc.—research reveals that their behaviors represent a consistent and logical use of the habits of their community rather than an *erroneous* or *underdeveloped* version of the "standard" language. The relatively simple yet important point here is that language variation is a logical and expected phenomenon; hence, we should not look upon nonstandard dialects as *deficient* versions of a language. English has a variety of dialects none of which is intrinsically any better than another; for social reasons we may call some "standard," or even "prestige," and others "nonstandard." Such reasons, or linguistic attitudes, are next discussed.

Attitudinal Correlates of Language

As research reveals well-defined differences in language behaviors for people from different social strata, it raises the question of whether these same differences can be identified by the everyday listener to such speech. Some researchers call this the "Pygmalion effect"—the degree to which a speaker's language characteristics enable people to judge his social status. Studies of this effect incorporate sociolinguistic variables—*viz.*, speakers, the linguistic variables on which the speakers vary, and the continuum of such variation as well as its relation to the speech situation. Also there is the identification of the type of listener being studied.

Social Status Attitudes

The study typically cited as evidence of listeners' ability to predict social status is one reported by Putnam and O'Hern (1955) which involved language samples from the Washington, D.C. area. The researchers found a relatively high correlation between the actual social status of the speakers and that guessed by listeners who had heard brief segments of the speech samples. Later another researcher (Harms, 1961, 1963) found that such status predictions could be made when listeners heard as few as ten to fifteen seconds of a speech sample.

Cultural Stereotypes

Well known studies of associations between language and cultural stereotypes have come from the work of Lambert and his colleagues (e.g., Lambert, Hodgson, Gardner, and Fillenbaum, 1960) who have had persons imagine the characteristics of persons speaking French or English. Unknown to the listeners was that the speakers of the two languages were actually the same people— perfect bilinguals. When listeners (bilingual Canadian university students) heard the samples they were asked to rate characteristics on such scales as height, good looks, leadership, sense of humor, intelligence, and the like. Even though they had been recorded by the same persons, the "speakers" in the English language versions were rated typically more favorably than in their French language versions. Such ratings were generally agreed upon by students from both the English and French Canadian communities.

The interpretation of the above research was that people associated language characteristics with cultural stereotypes. Presumably, then, a listener, upon hearing a few speech characteristics, could rapidly hypothesize a stereotype for the speaker in that speech situation.

Occupational Attitudes

Given the finding that selected phonological variables (discussed earlier) were associated with social stratification in New York City, Labov (1966) reasoned that these same variables should serve as cues to listeners in identifying the social status of the speaker's occupation.

Recordings of sentences were edited from tapes of speakers reading aloud a passage which in different segments had concentrations of each of the /r/, /æ/, /ɔ/, /ð/, and /θ/ variables from the stratification study. The speakers from different social strata used for recording the passage were known beforehand to vary as anticipated in their treatment of the variables.

When presented with playbacks of the tapes, listeners were asked to imagine themselves in the role of a personnel manager of a large corporation who was interviewing job candidates. Each speaker's tape was rated in terms of a continuum of occupations including (in order): "television personality, executive secretary, receptionist, switchboard operator, salesgirl, factory worker, and 'none of the above.' " The listener was to assign the speaker to the occupation for which his speech was most suited, the assumption being that the occupations defined an attitude scale ranging from "perfect" to "terrible" speech.

Results revealed differentiations that were very consistent among the listeners in rating the speech sounds on the occupational scale. Moreover, many of the occupational ratings could be interpreted as roughly parallel to the social variations found in the speakers sampled from the different social strata. In other words, the social stratification of the linguistic variables had interpretable correlates in how listeners assigned occupations to persons who spoke in ways characteristic of different strata.

Race and Status Identifications

In a study of attitudes toward Detroit speech, Shuy and his colleagues (Shuy, Baratz, and Wolfram, 1969), used brief (roughly thirty seconds) taped samples of Negro and White male speakers from different socioeconomic classes of the city. Individuals who heard and who answered questions about the tapes included grade school children and adults, Negroes and Whites, males and females, and persons from different social classes.

On the average, individuals were able to identify correctly about 30 % of the upper-middle class speakers; 32 % of the lower-middle class; 41 % of the upper-working class, and 61 % of the lower-working class. A generalization, then, was that the lower the socioeconomic class of a respondent the more his speech "marked" his social status. When examined from the social status of the listener, the researchers found that upper-middle class respondents were generally more accurate for different status identifications than were the lower-working class persons. However, all respondents were about equally good at identifying the lower-working class speakers.

Listeners were able to identify correctly the speech of Negroes in 80% of the judgments and Whites in 81%. These were for tapes ranging between twenty to thirty seconds' duration. With tapes of from three to five seconds each, accuracy was 70% for Negro speakers and 67% for Whites. Finally, the ethnic identifications were fairly close in percentage of correct responses in the comparison of White and Negro listeners' judgments.

Among the generalizations based upon the above findings, Shuy and his colleagues noted that it is the appearance of certain stigmatized grammatical and phonological features that marked the speech of the lower socioeconomic groups. The middle class speakers rather than having prestige features were identified by their lack of the stigmatized ones.

Teachers' Ratings of Children's Speech

Another type of attitude study (Williams, 1970) was an attempt to assess how teachers evaluated the speech of pupils, particularly in terms of their "sounding disadvantaged." Tapes of forty speech samples from fourth and fifth grade, Negro and White children, and males and females, sampled from low and middle income homes, were employed in the research. The tapes, averaging about four to five minutes in duration, were of the children responding to questions about television and about games that they played.

By a process of having teachers use speech rating scales, it was found that they tended to evaluate children's speech along two gross dimensions. One of these was labeled as *confidence-eagerness*, based upon the teachers' similar uses of individual scales reflecting fluency, enthusiasm, and amount of speech provided by the child in the interview. The second was labeled *ethnicity-non-standardness*, and was based upon such scales as pronunciation standardness, word usage, and sounding "ethnic."

In a subsequent phase of the research, it was found that the frequency of certain speech and language characteristics as tabulated for the tapes could be used to predict mathematically the ratings on the two dimensions. The best predictor of confidence-eagerness was the incidence of hesitation phenomena. This was an inverse relation; the fewer the hesitations the more confident-eager the child was rated. Ethnicity-nonstandardness was best predicted from the incidence of several nonstandardizations on the tapes—for example, "d" [d] for voiced "th" [ð] sounds, pronominal apposition ("The girl *she* came in"), and the like.

Finally, it was found that teachers' judgments of a child's "sounding disadvantaged" could be jointly predicted by the ratings of confidence-eagerness and ethnicity-nonstandardness. That is, teachers seemed to equate sounding disadvantaged with being reticent and unsure and with the use of English nonstandardizations.

A generalization derived from several of the foregoing studies is that just as language characteristics are found to be socially stratified, there is often a parallel in social attitudes associated with these characteristics. In many cases, the English language characteristics which are socially stratified and which serve as attitudinal cues are relatively insignificant linguistically. That is, for example, a "d" for "th" substitution or the like does not usually hinder a speaker's intelligibility. The variation is not significant enough to change the meaning of the utterance. On the other hand, such characteristics may be socially significant. That is, they may affect our attitudes toward the speaker and what he says. In this respect, such attitudes may well bias our interpretation of what we hear.

Some linguists have adopted the terms *acrolect* and *basilect* to refer to the highest and lowest prestige forms of a dialect. The features which vary between these extremes and their range of variation are akin to the earlier mentioned concepts of linguistic variable and linguistic continuum.

The Mode of Speech Concept

In the types of sociolinguistic study discussed thus far the linguistic variable has typically been defined in terms of detailed phonological or syntactic variations. Such studies have involved relatively traditional specifications of linguistic variables although the use of quantification has been a new addition. In contrast to this detailed type of specification is a broader concern with the general types of speech which are brought to bear to meet the communicative demands of speech situations. The exact description of the types of speech remains a problem in theorizing of this type. Generally, however, the term *mode of speech* has been used to denote this broader focus upon the roles of speech, speakers, and the communicative demands of speech situations.

Toward an Ethnography of Speaking

One approach to the level of study involved in modes of speech comes from the anthropologist Dell Hymes (especially, 1962) who has argued that we have too often failed to study the activity of speaking in its own right. He has called for the formalization of a method for such study and has labeled it an *ethnography of speaking*. In Hymes's (1962, p. 16) own terms:

> In one sense this area fills the gap between what is usually described in grammars, and what is usually described in ethnographies. Both use speech as evidence of other patterns; neither brings it into focus in terms of its own patterns. In another sense, this is a question of what a child internalizes about speaking, beyond rules of grammar and a dictionary, while becoming a full-fledged member of its speech community. Or, it is a question of what a foreigner must learn about a group's verbal behavior in order to participate appropriately and effectively in its activities. *The ethnography of speaking is concerned with the situations and uses, the patterns and functions, of speaking as an activity in its own right.* [italics added]

Speech situations. In our own society we have everyday names for kinds of speech events, and the range of circumstances denoted by these names suggests ways to classify speech situations. Consider, for example, such events as sales talks, bull sessions, polite conversation, griping, cocktail party chatter, job-interviewing, bargaining, lecturing, and so on. Each suggests some combination of speaker, listener, setting, topics, and the types of language demanded.

Modes of speech. If we try to classify general types of speech that involve entire patterns of usage in given situations, the concept of mode of speech becomes useful. Thus, for example, the *formal-informal* modes of speech were manipulated in the urban studies discussed earlier. Under appropriate circumstances, informants from the higher socioeconomic classes would engage in a formal mode sooner than would the lower status persons. Generally, a formal mode incorporates a range of features that identify it linguistically, including, for example, sentences which are more complex grammatically, as well as a low frequency of grammatical and phonological nonstandardizations. In terms of the *linguistic variable* concept mentioned earlier, a mode of speech is a definition of this variable in terms of multiple rather than individual linguistic features. Often, too, a mode of speech is identified according to a functional role in the speech situation.

The definition of the functional roles of speech is a matter of varying opinions. Hymes suggests that one basis for definition lies in how the language of a speech situation relates to different factors of that situation. For example:

> *Expressive*—relates to the speaker
> *Directive*—relates to the listener
> *Poetic*—relates to the message form itself
> *Contact*—relates to the communication channel
> *Metalinguistic*—relates to the language used
> *Referential*—relates to the message topic
> *Contextual*—relates to the speech situation

Obviously, most speech situations represent a combination of language functions, and these combinations may vary even within the sequence of a given situation.

As much as is possible, the ethnographer of speaking wishes to deal with (1) the definition of speech settings, (2) their constituent factors, and (3) the uses of speech relative to the social structures or societies of which the settings are a part. Presumably, every society can be assumed to have social structures and social roles which can be identified with types of speech situations. These situations have their related modes of speech which fulfill speech functions. The aim of such identifications and definitions is to characterize the "situations and uses, the patterns and functions, of speaking . . ." mentioned earlier.

Bernstein's Theorizing on Social Class Differences in Speech

The British sociologist, Basil Bernstein, has tried to initiate a way of answering a major sociolinguistic question: Why do groups, particularly of different social strata, tend to use language differently? Although Bernstein's (1970) research has not been undertaken precisely within the ethnographic framework suggested by Hymes, it does represent a type of theorizing done about modes of speech.

Restricted and elaborated language codes. Bernstein is mostly known for his observations and speculations concerning the concepts of *restricted* and *elaborated* language codes. Originally, this distinction was observed in the speech of British citizens of the lower ("working") and middle socioeconomic classes respectively.

The restricted code was a mode of speech observed in situations where speaker and listener presumably had a high degree of shared experience, thus allowing speech to be abbreviated and with more of an emphasis upon the social interaction of that situation than upon the communication of complex messages. To an observer, such speech, although fluent, would appear incomplete or truncated, with limited and often redundant linguistic choices. Meaning does not seem explicit in the language which is used. There is as much emphasis upon how something is said, as on what is said. The most typical use of this style of speech, or re-stricted code, is among persons who know one another (or their respective roles) very well, as between husband and wife, a G.I. and his peers, among the members of a youth gang, to name a few examples. The social linkage is as important as the topic of discourse.

The elaborated code does not require a high degree of shared experiences (save for linguistic knowledge) between speaker and listener. Through the use of detailed language, meaning is made explicit. To an observer, speech in the elaborate code would appear complete and typically rich in the choice of linguistic alter-natives. Examples of elaborated code would be a university lecture (sometimes!), a mother explaining reasons to her child for not eating between meals, formal argument, scientific description, and all such situations where discourse has a strong topic-centered component.

Another contrast between restricted and elaborated codes

is in the degree to which the message can transcend the communication context. To use an example of Bernstein's (1970, p. 26), note the contrast in the context-boundedness of the two following stories developed to describe the happenings shown in a four-picture sequence. The pictures begin with boys playing football near a house and end with a woman peering through a broken window.

> (elaborated) Three boys are playing football and one boy kicks the ball—and it goes through the window—the ball breaks the window—and the boys are looking at it—and a man comes out and shouts at them—because they've broken the window—so they run away—and then that lady looks out of her window—and she tells the boys off.

> (restricted) They're playing football—and he kicks it and it goes through there—it breaks the window and they're looking at it—and he comes out and shouts at them—because they've broken it—so they run away—and then she looks out and she tells them off.

Much of Bernstein's theorizing about the two codes is based upon his observations of how the British working class tends to employ mainly the restricted code, while the middle class tends to employ both codes.

Social roles and linguistic codes. In a more general vein Bernstein has proposed an association of restricted and elaborated codes with *closed* and *open* social-role systems.

Consider the types of social roles that humans assume in the family, in occupations, the military, school, church, and in other organized social structures. All such roles involve verbal coding activities. In fact the roles could be differentiated in terms of these activities. The encoding activities of two children are apt to be far more similar to each other than either child's activities are to the encoding behavior of their mother. Roles also vary in terms of the range of verbal alternatives associated with them. Thus the authority structure of the military depends upon orders given to subordinates by superiors. The subordinate's role is of a relatively *closed* type verbally; the role does not depend upon (in this sense at least) the exercise of a large range of verbal encoding alternatives. By contrast, the superior's role depends highly upon verbal activity. In this regard it is a verbally *open* role.

Although some roles represent typically closed or open verbal roles, other roles may vary, depending upon their particular circumstances. For example, a family may be characterized in terms of its degrees of openess as against closedness in the verbal roles its members fulfill. If family control, and hence communication, is mainly direction-giving (e.g., an authoritarian family structure) then verbal elaboration is not required, nor encouraged, among its members. Accordingly, its members may operate in generally closed social roles. By contrast, a family structure could also be made up of social roles that encourage verbalization of a wide range of alternatives, as in discussing decisions, reasons for direction-giving, and so on.

An obvious point is that the elaborated and restricted codes serve the open and closed social roles, respectively. Presumably, an individual grows into and maintains a variety of social roles. Some individuals may operate predominantly in a variety of closed roles and others in a mixture of open and closed roles. It is not unusual, then, for a person in the former category to grow into, and eventually become solely a user of, the restricted code.

Modes of social control. The types of social control used in open and closed roles are also illustrative of the association between social roles and the ranges of verbal alternatives employed in speech. An *imperative* mode involves the fewest linguistic alternatives. It involves commands or direction given by the speaker, either of which are realizable in the restricted code. It offers the respondent only the options of compliance or rejection. Moreover, it does not intentionally encourage verbal exchange by the listener (except perhaps for imperatives such as "Tell me," etc.). The imperative mode is characteristic of speech in closed social roles.

Appeals as modes of social control are divided by Bernstein into two categories: *positional* and *personal*. Positional appeals, as the label implies, are directed to the rules or expectations associated with social roles rather than to the individual concerns of the persons serving in those roles. Personal appeals are focused upon people in the roles, as in appealing to an individual's sense of reason for an action or belief.

Suppose, for example, a small child is headed for the cookie jar. Trying to stop him by using the imperative mode would be represented by such utterances as "No!," "Get away," and so on. A positional appeal would be: "Good boys don't eat cookies before supper." A personal appeal would be "Don't eat a cookie now because it will spoil your appetite for supper." Depending upon the verbal elaboration involved, positional and personal appeals may be in restricted or elaborated codes.

Linguistic socialization. A major thesis within Bernstein's theorizing is that the learning of restricted, elaborated, or both of the codes is a major way by which social structures perpetuate themselves in the children of parents from those structures. That is, a social structure is manifest in a family structure and in the constituent roles people take within it. As children are reared to assume these roles they learn the associated linguistic code and this learning transmits the social structure to the new generation. Children typically grow up in social environments which stress certain modes of social control. Such stress has consequences upon what a child learns about himself relative to the social structure. The imperative mode, for example, stresses authority as it exists in the social role hierarchy. Positional appeals teach role expectations and obligations. Personal appeals stress a type of independence from social role, as in being an "individual."

A key point is that mode of social control, social role, and linguistic code tend to vary together. Families may have closed social roles, typically use the imperative and positional-appeal modes of control, and do most of this in the restricted code. A child reared in the environment may be equipped to deal with open roles, particularly as the roles involve personal appeals and elaborated codes. This, according to Bernstein, is the working class child's problem in Great Britain. He has been so thoroughly socialized into the restricted code in his preschool years, that the elaborated code requirements of the school are irrelevant if not frustrating to him.

Application in the United States. Some persons (e.g., Deutsch et al., 1967) have applied Bernstein's restricted code distinction to the lower socioeconomic classes in the United States, particularly to the so-called "disadvantaged" among inner-city populations. Such applications have made a hasty identification between a kind of deficit or underdeveloped language diagnosis of the American who speaks a nonstandard dialect of English and Bernstein's concept of a restricted code. The problem with this identification, according to Bernstein (1970), is that the restricted code does not imply a linguistic underdevelopment—for indeed, the language of children in these populations has developed quite normally to meet the demands of a child's social role. Also the linguistic picture in the United States often has an ethnic group differentiation in addition to social dialect differentiation among socially stratified groups. Thus the distinction between restricted and elaborated codes as observed among English-speaking groups in Great Britain may be considerably modified in the United States where groups may further vary in terms of having Negro dialect or even Spanish as a primary language. In short, the applicability of Bernstein's thesis in the United States remains a research question even though various researchers (e.g., Deutsch, et al., 1967; Hess and Shipman, 1965, 1968), including the author (Williams and Naremore, 1969a, b), have speculated on the topic.

Sociolinguistic Development

In the final section of Chapter 5 we discussed the contemporary psycholinguistic perspective on the development of language in children. One main assumption was that the child had a biological endowment which would "program" the developmental sequence. From the linguistic competency standpoint, the acquisitional sequence was seen as the child's development of linguistic knowledge. This development presumably results from the interaction of biological and social factors. The biological factors define the capability for inducing and internalizing linguistic knowledge from linguistic experiences. The social factors define these experiences. In this section we will discuss theoretical and research perspectives, a topic which, in contrast to the concept of *developmental psycholinguistics* introduced in Chapter 5, might be labeled, *developmental sociolinguistics*.

General Perspectives

As mentioned in the discussion of Bernstein's theorizing, some of the attention to social factors in language development has been in terms of social class or socioeconomic differences in children's language performances. Perhaps the best known major studies of such differences in America are those by McCarthy (1930) and Templin (1957). Both McCarthy and Templin studied relatively large groups of children in terms of their performances in articulating English sounds, creating certain syntactic patterns, and so on. Despite the wealth of information made available in these studies, it is important to remember that they focused upon performance in standard-English-speaking situations and, of course, gauged performance in terms of standard English criteria. As we have seen in the social dialect research of Labov and Shuy, however, the correlations between social class and language performance in such studies may reflect more of a correlation with standard English performance than with language development per se. Accordingly, the question then is: How can we describe development in a relative sense—that is, how can we view a child's development in his own speech community, and in ways not biased by cultural or subcultural differences between the child and the assessment techniques?

Current theorizing suggests two answers to the above question. First, we should conduct developmental studies using the approach of the anthropologist whereby subcultures or cultures are studied in and of themselves, and not just relative to some criterion culture. Or in more practical terms, we need to study language development in a way as free as possible from our own (i.e., the researcher's) cultural biases. Second, if we are interested in making subcultural or cultural comparisons about language development, we should try to identify those behaviors that represent the most universal aspects of the acquisition sequence.

Research Methods

Although this chapter is largely restricted to sociolinguistic study within subcultures or cultures, it is important to consider culture-free methods for studying language acquisition. The most promising ideas for such study have been outlined by Slobin and his colleagues (1967). In specifying the major topics for investigation, the researchers differentiated between psycholinguistic topics and sociolinguistic ones. The former referred to indexes of phonologic, syntactic, and vocabulary development, the latter to what they called *communicative development*.

In the examples which follow, all test topics and methods are presumed to be relevant across different speech communities. Although the structure (*how* something is said) of expression may vary drastically, the linguistic capability (*what* is said) is universal. For example, that children reach a stage of associating minimum sounds with distinctions in meanings (phonemitization) is a developmental universal. Or a child's capability to comprehend or produce pluralization is relevant to all speech communities. Even the general needs that humans have in adapting their speech to the demands of communication situations—for example, greetings, questions, arguing, telling jokes—appear to be relevant cross-culturally. Following are some examples of psycholinguistic and sociolinguistic topics from Slobin, et al. (1967). Again, these are topics thought to have generality across cultures.

Psycholinguistic topics. Study of phonologic development is focused upon the stages of: (1) *cooing*, (generally pleasurable vowel-like vocalizations with no systematic repetitions of individual sounds), (2) *babbling* (includes consonant-like sounds, gives impression of syllabic repetition), and (3) *speech* (phonemic use of sounds; i.e., a consistent sound-meaning relationship). Since the study of children's total vocabularies would be a monumental undertaking, interest was focused upon *initial vocabulary*. What are a child's first words? What semantic domains (classes of referents) do these words cover, or do not cover? What kinds of meaning generalizations are associated with initial vocabulary items? What is the extent of homonymity (words sounding alike but with different meanings)? What are the apparent grammatical categories of the words?

Grammatical assessment generally concerns the syntactic patterns and functions of word sequences, primarily as a child may be able to imitate, comprehend, or freely produce such sequences. Sentence imitation provides a means for examining whether or how a child can replicate the syntactic structures administered by the researcher. Presumably, the more closely a child can reproduce the original structure, the more it indicates that he possesses the grammatical knowledge needed to comprehend and create that structure. Test items are often too difficult to simply "parrot" and intonation will usually reveal such parroting as compared to a comprehension and recoding of the item. Moreover, the types of errors (word changes, omissions, etc.) a child makes can be interpreted as symptomatic of the type of grammatical knowledge the child lacks or has failed to use.

Comprehension assessment is done using techniques where pictures or objects illustrate a grammatical distinction in a test utterance. For example, given two pictures where one shows only a single kitten and the other shows two, a child can be asked to point to, or pick up, the picture that goes with the sentence, "The kittens play." An example of object manipulation as a test of comprehension could be to present the child with a penny and a plate, then give him a variety of instructions such as: "Put the penny on the plate." "Put the penny under the plate," and so on. The crucial feature of such comprehension assessments is that the sentence and the pictures or objects involve the unambiguous test of a specific grammatical distinction. An obvious problem is that some grammatical distinctions do not lend themselves to unambiguous portrayal.

Speech production as elicited by other methods than imitation often involves a compromise between trying to control precisely what production is to be tested as against trying to encourage the child to speak freely and then assess what he happens to say. Controlled test methods include such techniques as eliciting a child's use of specific grammatical rules. A well-known example is the Berko (1958) test item where a child is shown a single sketch of a bird-like animal and is told: "This is a wug." Next he sees a sketch with two of the animals and is told: "Now there is another one; there are two of them." Then he is asked to complete the sentence: "There are two——." Presumably, if the child says "wug*s*," he has used his knowledge of the noun plural inflection in English as it is applied to a morpheme ending in a stop consonant. Other controlled methods include setting up situations involving dolls where the researcher starts a conversational situation between the dolls—perhaps involving a specific verb tense—then has the child provide parts of that conversation.

Sociolinguistic topics. An obvious necessity in describing the environmental influences on a child is to have a systematic way to identify and classify such influences. Slobin, et al. (1967) calls this the description of a child's *lifespace*. For individual children this includes such factors as the characteristics of the child's household, its physical setting, and the persons who comprise the household. A second cluster of factors center upon caretaking: who has what social (and parental) relations with the child? Finally, there is the specification of linguistic inputs: who talks to the child about what, and in what settings, and so on?

As compared with psycholinguistic assessment, which often lends itself to experimental manipulations of the child's verbal behavior, sociolinguistic assessment is typically more descriptive. Given the child's so-called lifespace, a key task is to describe it carefully. Manipulating it may change the circumstances the researcher is trying to study. Within the lifespace there are potentially identifiable categories of language behavior that seem useful to assess in most cultures. One of these is the variation observed in children as they talk to one another, particularly as the children differ in age.

Another sociolinguistic focus is in parental babytalk, which seems to be found in most cultures. Consonant clusters are often simplified, grammar is simplified, and vocabulary, as might be expected, predominates in the referents of the child's lifespace (e.g., kin names, nicknames, body parts, animals, toys, etc.).

Part of a child's verbal activity occurs in situations where what is said is highly predictable; these behaviors are called *routines.* Examples are situation-boundary-markers (greetings, farewells, etc.); accident-markers (saying something after sneezing, tripping, etc.); apologies; thanks; and gesture-word-games (the verbal accompaniment of playing "peek-a-boo", "patty-cake", etc.).

Societies seem to have rules for conversational interactions, and children must learn these rules. These include verbal strategies for initiating or ending a conversation, recognition of taboo words or topics, shifting the perspective of the speaker (as in shifting from first to third person constructions), introduction of new terms or items, dialect choice and shifting, and methods for constructing narrative sequences, to name a few.

Relations of Form and Function in Language

From the foregoing list of topics it should be apparent that psycholinguistic and sociolinguistic topics inextricably overlap. Thus it is one thing for a child to learn the rules for the creation (generation) of noun phrases, but he also learns when and how to use these phrases in his practical communication behaviors. It seems reasonable to assume that the development of form and function go together in language behavior and acquisition. Table 6.1 outlines this speculation in more detail relative to three main modes of speech: context-centered, sender/receiver-centered, and topic-centered. In table 6.1 note how the demands upon form vary from the most simple in context-centered speech to the most complex in topic-centered speech. These extremes and their functional correlates represent distinctions similar to Bernstein's contrasts between restricted and elaborated codes, only the present scheme is more a continuum than a dichotomy of these contrasts. The roles of nonverbal communication (gestures, facial expression) can also be seen in this continuum. In context-centered speech, nonverbal forms can often take the place of verbal ones, whereas in topic-centered speech, nonverbal forms only complement what is said verbally. Most speech behaviors of the impulsive and contactive types in context-centered communication require no syntactic capabilities, yet topic-centered speech not only relies heavily upon syntactic alternatives but upon strategies for overall message organization. Like Bernstein's code distinctions, speech in context-centered situations would often be ambiguous if interpreted outside of context; however, topic-centered speech should be largely context-free in its interpretation.

The kinds of speech situations described in table 6.1 can easily be found in the discourse of children. In fact these descriptions were drawn from a study of American children of different ethnicities, sex, and social classes (Williams and Naremore, 1969a, b). A question is whether the range of speech types from those of context-centered to topic-centered represent a developmental continuum. That is, do children start out with context-centered speech, then eventually add sender/receiver and topic-centered speech types to their repertoires? Also, if child language development does progress in terms of these combinations of form and function, are form and function two aspects of the same capability or knowledge? Does one precede the other in development? Are they separate entities? Such questions remain for research.

Communicative competence. One current thought is that the development of function and form are so closely tied as to make relevant a single concept called *communicative competence* (Hymes, 1970). As Chomsky characterized a person's grammatical knowledge in terms of *linguistic competence*, the concept of communicative

Table 6.1 Intersections of language form and function in different speech situations (from Frederick Williams and Rita C. Naremore, "On the Functional Analysis of Social Class Differences in Modes of Speech," *Speech Monographs*, 36, (1969): 98. Reprinted by permission).

Modes	Function	Form	Examples
IMPULSIVE (context-centered)	Utterance bound to contextual factors. Receiver and topic are irrelevant.	Typically very minimal forms, even those which are vocal and nonverbal (e.g., a scream). Single words, no syntactic requirements. Many forms could be expressed nonvocally through facial and gestural expressions.	"ouch," "wow" "oh," "ah," screaming, laughter, crying, swearing etc.
CONTACTIVE (context-centered)	Utterances reflect upon the sender's attempt to initiate, evaluate, or maintain linkage with a receiver or receivers. Topic is irrelevant.	Minimal word forms, even where meaning is insignificant. Minimal phrase constructs, stereotyped in structure, syntactic distinctions insignificant. Some forms could be expressed nonverbally (hand waving).	"hello," "hey," "John?" "waiter!" "How do you do?" "you know," "do you hear me?"
CONVERSATIVE (context-centered)	Utterances reinforce and maintain linkage with receiver. Topic may be relevant, but is seen more in the context of the discourse than in the speech of an individual.	Minimal word forms and syntactic fragments allowable, but can range to relatively developed sequences. Typically complemented by nonverbal forms.	cocktail party chatter, language exchanged between persons just introduced, elaborated greetings and farewells, simple yes-no answers. names, etc.

Modes	Function	Form	Examples
DESCRIPTIVE DIRECTIVE (sender or receiver centered)	Topic is relevant as the object of discourse, but elaboration, if any, is through reference to concrete and particular experiences. Description reveals such experience from a sender-centered perspective, whereas direction prescribes an experience for the receiver's actions.	Minimal word forms and syntactic fragments are allowable for naming or commands, but syntactic elaboration is required to verbally symbolize the structure of the experience. Illustrative gesturing may serve as rudimentary forms or to complement verbal elaborations. Elaboration depends upon expansion of predicate phrase structures.	Recounting some event which has been experienced; delineating in verbal terms a "picture" of something; telling a person how to play a game, step-by-step; giving instructions to a traveller; commanding some action.
ELABORATIVE (topic centered)	Topic is explicitly relevant as the object of discourse, and such discourse may be adapted to the perceptions of the receiver, including distinctions among either individual receivers or groups of receivers. Explicit topical elaboration reaches to levels which can only be obtained through verbal symbolism. Primarily a topical mode.	Demands are imposed for maximal lexical and syntactic alternatives. The structure of discourse is achieved through syntactic and compositional features which are organizing devices in themselves and are not dependent upon the reference to concrete experience. Nonverbal forms are minimally relevant at this level.	Interpretation, or explaining one's understanding of the meaning of some event which has been experienced, or of some concept or idea (e.g., what "freedom" means). Narration, or developing a topic in story form (e.g., retelling the story of a movie or TV show). Persuasion, or inducing direction in thinking or behavior by overt verbal appeal (e.g., a mother reasoning with her child).

competence incorporates with linguistic competence, knowledge of a sociolinguistic nature. In Hymes' (in prep.) own terms:

> The acquisition of competency for use, indeed, can be stated in the same terms as acquisition of competence for grammar. Within the developmental matrix in which knowledge of the sentences of a language is acquired, children also acquired knowledge of a set of ways in which sentences are used. From a finite experience of speech acts and their interdependence with sociocultural features they develop a general theory of the speaking appropriate in their community, which they employ, like other forms of tacit cultural knowledge (competence) in conducting and interpreting social life.

If it seems a large order for the child to develop his capabilities for creating and understanding the sentences of his language, it seems an equally large order that he also learn when and how to use these sentences. Currently, we have only the beginnings of research into the sociolinguistic aspects of language. What seems ironic is that although we average fifteen hours of our day typically engaged in the everyday use of language, it is this use that we seem to know the least about.

References

BERKO, J., "The Child's Learning of English Morphology," *Word*, 14, (1958), 150–77.

BERNSTEIN, B., "A Sociolinguistic Approach to Socialization: With Some Reference to Educability," in *Language and Poverty: Perspectives on a Theme*, ed. F. Williams. Chicago: Markham, 1970.

BEVER, T. G., "The Cognitive Basis for Linguistic Structures," in *Cognition and the Development of Language*, ed. J. R. Hayes. New York: Wiley, 1970.

BLOOM, L., *Language Development: Form and Function in Emerging Grammars*. Cambridge, Mass.: M.I.T. Press, 1970.

BROWN, R., and U. BELLUGI, "Three Processes in the Child's Acquisition of Syntax," *Harvard Educational Review*, 34, (1964), 133–51.

CAZDEN, C., "Environmental Assistance to the Child's Acquisition of Grammar." Unpublished doctoral dissertation, Harvard University, 1965.

CHOMSKY, N., *Syntactic Structures*. The Hague: Mouton, 1957.

CHOMSKY, N., "Review of B. F. Skinner's *Verbal Behavior*," *Language*, 35, (1959), 26–58.

———, *Aspects of the Theory of Syntax*. Cambridge, Mass.: M.I.T. Press, 1965.

———, and M. HALLE, *The Sound Pattern of English*. New York: Harper, 1968.

DEUTSCH, M., and associates, *The Disadvantaged Child*. New York: Basic Books, 1967.

FODOR, J. A., and M. GARRETT, "Some Reflections on Competence and Performance," in *Psycholinguistic Papers, Proceedings of the Edinburgh Conference*, eds. J. Lyons and R. J. Wales. Chicago: Aldine, 1966.

———, and M. GARRETT, "Some Syntactic Determinants of Sentential Complexity," *Perception and Psychophysics*, 2, (1967), 289–96.

GLEASON, H. A., Jr., *An Introduction to Descriptive Linguistics*. New York: Holt, Rinehart and Winston, 1961.

GLEASON, H. A., JR., *Linguistics and English Grammar.* New York: Holt, Rinehart and Winston, 1965.

HARMS, L. S., "Listener Judgments of Status Cues in Speech," *Quarterly Journal of Speech*, 47, (1961), 164–68.

——, "Status Cues in Speech: Extra-race and Extra-region Identification," *Lingua*, 12, (1963), 300–306.

HESS, R. D., and V. SHIPMAN, "Early Blocks to Children's Learning," *Children*, 12, (1965), 189–94.

——, and V. SHIPMAN, "Maternal Influences upon Early Learning: The Cognitive Environments of Urban Pre-school Children," in *Early Education: Current Theory, Research, and Action*, eds. R. D. Hess and R. M. Bear. Chicago: Aldine, 1968.

HOCKETT, C. F., *A Course in Modern Linguistics.* New York: Macmillan, 1958.

HYMES, D., "The Ethnography of Speaking," in *Anthropology and Human Behavior*, eds. T. Gladwin and W. C. Sturtevant. Washington, D.C.: Anthropological Society of Washington, 1962.

——, *On Communicative Competence*, in preparation.

JAKOBSON, R., "Kindersprache, aphasie, und allgemeine lautgesetze." Uppsala: Universitets Aarsskrift, 1941.

KATZ, J. J., and J. A. FODOR, "The Structure of a Semantic Theory," *Language*, 39, (1963), 170–210.

LABOV, W., *The Social Stratification of English in New York City.* Washington, D.C.: Center for Applied Linguistics, 1966.

LAMBERT, W. E., R. C. HODGSON, R. C. GARDNER, and S. FILLENBAUM, "Evaluational Reactions to Spoken Languages," *Journal of Abnormal and Social Psychology*, 60, (1960), 44–51.

LENNEBERG, E. H., *Biological Foundations of Language.* New York: Wiley, 1967.

McCAFFREY, A. R., "Speech Perception by Infants." Unpublished doctoral dissertation, Cornell University, 1969.

McCARTHY, D., *The Language Development of the Preschool Child.* Minneapolis: Univ. of Minnesota Press, 1930.

McNEILL, D., "Developmental Psycholinguistics," in *The Genesis of Language: A Psycholinguistic Approach*, eds. F. Smith and G. A. Miller. Cambridge, Mass.: M.I.T. Press, 1966.

——, *The Acquisition of Language: The Study of Developmental Psycholinguistics.* New York: Harper and Row, 1970.

MEHLER, J., "Some Effects of Grammatical Transformations on the Recall of English Sentences," *Journal of Verbal Learning and Verbal Behavior*, 2, (1963), 346–51.

MILLER, G. A., "Some Psychological Studies of Grammar," *American Psychologist*, 17, (1962), 748–62.

MILLER, G. A., "Some Preliminaries to Psycholinguistics," *American Psychologist*, 20, (1965), 15–20.

———, and N. CHOMSKY, "Finitary Models of Language Users," in *Handbook of Mathematical Psychology*, eds. R. D. Luce, R. Bush, and E. Galanter. New York: Wiley, 1963.

———, and K. McKEAN, "A Chronometric Study of Some Relations between Sentences," *Quarterly Journal of Experimental Psychology*, 16, (1964), 297–308.

MOFFITT, A. R., "Speech Perception by Infants." Unpublished doctoral dissertation, Univ. of Minnesota, 1969.

OSGOOD, C. E., "On Understanding and Creating Sentences," *American Psychologist*, 18, (1963), 735–51. .

PUTNAM, G. N., and E. O'HERN, "The Status Significance of an Isolated Urban Dialect," *Language*, 31, (1955), 1–32.

SAVIN, H., and E. PERCHONOCK, "Grammatical Structures and the Immediate Recall of English Sentences," *Journal of Verbal Learning and Verbal Behavior*, 4, (1965), 348–53.

SEVERSON, R. A., and K. E. GUEST, "Toward the Standardized Assessment of the Language of Disadvantaged Children," in *Language and Poverty: Perspectives on a Theme*, ed. F. Williams. Chicago: Markham, 1970.

SHUY, R. W., J. C. BARATZ, and W. A. WOLFRAM, "Sociolinguistic Factors in Speech Identification." N.I.M.H. Research Project No. MH-15048-01, Center for Applied Linguistics, 1969.

———, W. A. WOLFRAM, and W. K. RILEY, "Linguistic Correlates of Social Stratification in Detroit Speech." U.S.O.E. Cooperative Research Project No. 6-1347, Michigan State University, 1967.

SKINNER, B. F., *Verbal Behavior*. New York: Appleton-Century-Crofts, 1957.

SLOBIN, D. I., and others, "A Field Manual for Cross-Cultural Study of the Acquisition of Communicative Competence." (Mimeo). Berkeley, Calif.: Univ. of California, 1967.

SPRADLIN, J. R., "Environmental Factors and the Language Development of Retarded Children," in *Developments in Applied Psycholinguistics Research*, eds. S. Rosenberg and J. H. Koplin. New York: Macmillan, 1968.

STREET, J. C., "Methodology in Immediate Constituent Analysis," in *Approaches in Linguistic Methodology*, eds. I. Rauch and C. T. Scott. Madison Wis.: Univ. of Wisconsin Press, 1967.

TEMPLIN, M. C., *Certain Language Skills in Children, Their Development and Interrelationships*. Minneapolis: Univ. of Minnesota Press, 1957.

WILLIAMS, F., "Psychological Correlates of Speech Characteristics: On Sounding 'disadvantaged,' *Journal of Speech and Hearing Research*, 13, (1970), 472–88.

WILLIAMS, F., and R. C. NAREMORE, "On the Functional Analysis of Social Class Differences in Modes of Speech," *Speech Monographs*, 36, (1969), 77–102. (a)

———, and R. C. NAREMORE, "Social Class Differences in Children's Syntactic Performance: A Quantitative Analysis of Field Study Data," *Journal of Speech and Hearing Research*, 12, (1969), 777–93. (b)

| Index